AIRWAR: VOLUME III

AIRWAR: VOLUME III

OUTRAGED SKIES

EDWARD JABLONSKI

DOUBLEDAY & COMPANY, INC., GARDEN CITY, NEW YORK

ISBN: 0-385-04156-X
Library of Congress Catalog Card Number 72–134086
Copyright © 1971 by Edward Jablonski
9   8   7   6

For my friends,
CLAIRE and PETER CLAY
once of the hospitable "George II,"
Luton, Bedfordshire, and now
of the "Coach and Horses," Rickmansworth,
Hertfordshire, England.

Man, have pity on man.
Rain from the outraged sky
drowned the innocent earth
yet the seed did not die.
Flowering from that rebirth,
man, have pity on man
as you hold the fire in your hand
that can destroy mankind
and desolate every land.
If the power and the glory is this,
a flame that burns to the bone,
what shall be left to grow
when you and your fires have gone?
What maimed and desolate few
shall recover life's full span
from among the ashes of time?
Man, have pity on man.
                    Ursula Vaughan Williams

Contents

Preface

For many months, while the war raged in Europe—only in the air until after D-Day—the war in the Pacific seemed practically a matter of marking time. Not, of course, to those who were there, for in the exotic further reaches of the Pacific Theater of Operations, they lived a hellish existence and fought under frightful and frightening conditions.

Roosevelt and Churchill agreed at their "Arcadia" Conference held in Washington in the latter days of 1941 that the Grand Strategy would be aimed at "getting Hitler first." While the Japanese had struck an impressive blow and in time permeated a large area of the Pacific, the Arcadia agreement recognized the futility of trying to fight two wars simultaneously (as Hitler himself had so stupidly chosen to do); the Japanese were spread all over the Pacific, but Hitler was concentrated in Europe.

At the same time, however, the Japanese would have to be contained and someone would have to contain them; to a great extent, the Pacific became primarily an American problem—with, of course, the incomparable aid of Australian and New Zealand troops. To those sent to the Pacific, that was the Big War and, uninformed as they were about Grand Strategies, they found it difficult to understand why they were low men on the military totem pole. Supplies, replacements, parts, small luxuries seemed always in short supply. Planes and men literally fell apart.

All glamour was quickly stripped from the island paradises of the Pacific; the fighting ability of the Japanese soldier became a legend: He was mysterious, nearly invincible, and strangely indifferent to death. This was frightening, at first, and there were brave men who ran from this kind of fanatic warrior in the confusion of battle.

The fighting men—and this was true of both antagonists—were also, in a sense, victims of the power and personality struggles of their own leaders. This was especially marked in the Pacific, where MacArthur's headquarters seethed with intrigue and animosity; to this was added the further complication of the division of authority between the Army and the Navy. The war in the air over the Pacific was even further entangled because MacArthur's Chief of Staff simply did not like airmen. After all, they had all been kicked out of the Philippines, the Netherlands East Indies, and other points, so what good were they? They were a bunch of lighthearted kids who used up their expensive airplanes and who flouted every form of military propriety and dress; they were not "good soldiers." It took a hard little airman named Kenney to revise this attitude toward the kid fliers in his command and to teach the brass, earthbound as they were, how to make war in the air. In doing this he also taught the Japanese a thing or two.

Kenney's warring was for a time a kind of improvisation, as he used whatever he could get his hands on to keep going; when things turned against the Japanese, Kenney had himself an air force and a well-knit, disciplined army of kids. Although a great deal of bitter ground fighting occurred in New Guinea, much of the victory could be credited to Kenney's wily employment of air power.

Even after the tide had turned, the war in the Pacific was not over. The Battle of Midway took place in June of 1942, after which it was impossible for Japan ever to win the war; perhaps, but it continued for three long, life-consuming years. The first step on the road back was initiated by the Marines at Guadalcanal two months after Midway. It was called Operation Shoestring by the men who fought it, with good reason; they fought with very little, at times with aircraft that had no right to be in the sky, just as had the Air Force out of Australia and New Guinea.

The Pacific presented a unique battleground, consisting as it did of so much water; it was here that the aircraft carrier came into its own. By the time these appeared in numbers in the Pacific it was the Japanese airman who was forced to operate under terrible conditions. They too were worn out (to a greater degree than American pilots ever were) and their planes were pushed beyond normal usage. As fresh American airmen, with new planes in great numbers, appeared, tired or poorly trained Japanese pilots in used-up planes suffered. They too should not have been in the air. It was this that made a Marianas "Turkey Shoot," however unpredictable, inevitable.

This third volume in the series entitled *Airwar* attempts to present the story of the early fighting over the Pacific, to give some idea of what it was like to fight a poor man's war in an area rich in handicaps, problems, and unpredictability—not the least of which were human.

Considering the vasty distances, the Pacific war was fought on a small scale, until the war in Europe took its positive turn. It was a war of hit-and-run dogfights and, for a time, meager bombing missions; it was not at all a textbook war.

EDWARD JABLONSKI

OUTRAGED
SKIES

BOOK I
Kenney's Kids

This was the type of strategy we hated most. The Americans attacked and seized, with minimum losses, a relatively weak area, constructed air fields, and then proceeded to cut supply lines to our troops in that area.

—GENERAL MATSUIOCHI INO

Because of the food shortage, some companies have been eating the flesh of Australian soldiers. The taste is said to be good.

—LIEUTENANT SAKAMOTO

I

BUCCANEER

THE Pacific theater of operations offered an infinity of vista: great stretches of water and curving horizons, broken only by jungle-gnarled islands, coruscated atolls, and palm-fringed islets. There was more water than land and more sky than either. Clearly it was not a setting for massive land battles, such as Europe was, and distance precluded the strategic bombardment of the Japanese homeland. Instead, until air bases could be established within range of Japan, a series of contained, savage land battles must be fought, along with far-flung naval engagements and air battles. The deeper strategy lay in eliminating Japanese air power, in order to permit Allied naval and ground troops to function.

At Midway it had been revealed, to those receptive to revelation, that the war in the Pacific would be dominated, even resolved, by aircraft and not the battleship. Classic sea-borne warfare by the books was finished in the Pacific no less than land war in Europe. Those who clung to the old concepts were committed to certain defeat. Midway had proved this; but if it had proved that Japan could no longer win the Pacific war, that the end was not immediately in view was equally certain.

The United States Navy coveted all that Pacific water, and with its triumph through carrier aviation at Midway, it had raised its eyes to the heavens also. The Navy was most anxious to avenge Pearl

General Douglas MacArthur, General Sir Thomas Blamey, commander of Australian ground forces in the Southwest Pacific, and MacArthur's Chief of Staff, Lieutenant General Richard K. Sutherland. Before Kenney could feel he rightfully commanded MacArthur's air force, he found he had to come to a proper understanding with Sutherland, who, though he brilliantly served MacArthur, liked having his finger in every pie—including Kenney's air forces. Kenney, putting his cards on the table in characteristic out-in-the-open manner, emerged as the only and full commander of the air forces in the Southwest Pacific—and remained as such for the rest of the war.

(U. S. ARMY)

Curtiss C-46 "Commando" of Air Transport Command flying over "the Hump" between India and China. Not only were the U.S. air forces and the RAF in- *volved in fighting the Japanese in the air, the problem of supplies of the entire China-Burma-India theater was solved by air.* (U. S. AIR FORCE)

Harbor, hoping to assume full strategic control of the Pacific. Therein lay sufficient fuel for interservice argument, with enough remaining for international disagreements as well. The British had their hands full in the China-Burma-India theater, what with personal intrigues and a complex supply problem; in China proper Chennault continued to have to make do with what little he could get from the United States and the even less he received from Chiang Kai-shek. These theaters were preponderantly land masses and the problem of their internal politics interfered only indirectly with the Pacific.

All that stood between the U. S. Navy and full

control of the Pacific was General Douglas MacArthur. After enduring the ignominy of being booted out of the Philippines, the patrician, vain, and egocentric MacArthur found small consolation in being given half command of a second-rate war. MacArthur's share of the theater, called the Southwest Pacific Area, included, running southward, those regions in Japanese hands, the Philippines, Borneo, Celebes, New Guinea (the northern coast of which in time was overrun also), and the great subcontinent of Australia, which lay in the path of the invaders and where MacArthur languished, awaiting definition of his command.

The remainder of the Pacific "belonged" to Admiral Chester W. Nimitz, based at Pearl Harbor. A line running north and south, eventually along the 159th meridian just east of Australia cut through the Solomon Islands, skirting one of the southernmost of the group, Guadalcanal (which placed it technically under naval jurisdiction), while leaving the largest island, Bougainville (in the north) under MacArthur's jurisdiction. The definition of command became at times rather hazy, if not heated. In their respective theaters, MacArthur and Nimitz were absolute monarchs commanding all forces, naval, ground, and air. Where the battle lines merged or overlapped, the question of jurisdiction must be decided by co-operation, which was not always readily forthcoming in the scramble for supplies, men, matériel, and power.

Where MacArthur was motivated by a histrionic sense of his position in history, Nimitz was a cool professional Navy man who aimed for as much co-operation as possible. MacArthur's real naval bête noire was Admiral Ernest J. King, Chief of Naval Operations, Commander in Chief, United States Navy. King, blunt, decisive, brilliant—as was MacArthur—viewed the war from the standpoint of the United States Navy. Not only did this earn him the enmity of such men as Churchill (a navy man himself), but of a host of U. S. Army, Air Force, and Navy men as well.

MacArthur suspected King's Pacific planning was a personal vendetta out of Washington. That Europe was the favored battleground in 1942 was but another unfortunate sting, for the supplies required for MacArthur's avowed return to the Philippines were drained away. Isolated as he was in Australia, MacArthur pondered the defense of that great land mass with few troops, a worn-out and he believed a "disloyal" air force, and little hope of acquiring the means and the men to turn the losing defensive war into the offensive.

MacArthur assumed command of the Southwest Pacific Area on April 18, 1942. "None of the three elements of my command—naval, air or ground—was adequate " he said. He had left more troops in the Philippines than he had at his disposal in Australia, and these were either the remnants of the fighting which had gone before or green troops, ill-equipped and poorly trained. His small naval detachment had no carriers. His air force, commanded by Lieutenant General George H. Brett, was little more than a ragtag of P-40s, P-400s (an early export model of the Bell P-39, Airacobra), P-39s, and a few worn-out B-17s, the even more worn Douglas A-24s (the Air Force version of the Navy's Dauntless) which were joined later by a trickle of B-25s and B-26s.

Brett was not regarded by MacArthur as one of the loyal ones (primarily because Brett did not get along with MacArthur's Chief of Staff, Major General Richard K. Sutherland). As far as the entire Air Force was concerned, MacArthur was certain it would contribute little to the war. Brett and MacArthur were thoroughly estranged, and Sutherland by no means eased the situation. Sutherland, in fact, enjoyed the position of all but running the show and, as described by an old classmate of his at the Army War College, "rubbed people the wrong way. He was egotistic, like most people, but an unfortunate bit of arrogance combined with his egotism had made him almost universally disliked."

From Australia MacArthur hoped to lunge northward via New Guinea, at the great Japanese base at Rabaul, in New Britain. From Rabaul, Japanese fighters and bombers were positioned to sweep down into New Guinea to attack the major Allied base at Port Moresby, to initiate the assault upon Australia. On the other hand, the Navy had its attention drawn to the Solomons, where great activity on Guadalcanal made it obvious that the Japanese were constructing an air base there. From the Solomons, by bombing Allied bases in the New Hebrides and New Caledonia, the Japanese could eventually cut the supply lines to Australia as well as the South Pacific. From air fields in the Solomons also the Japanese could protect Rabaul, with its concentration of ships and aircraft.

Brett had much to contend with as the commander of the Allied Air Forces in the Southwest Pacific besides Sutherland. His personality, a mingling of hauteur and ego, caused trouble too. Brett could not bring himself to warm up to the Australians, particularly with its governmental representatives, members of a "radical" Labour government and therefore "left wing." The problem of replacement and supply was formidable and the morale of exhausted crews was low. Fatigued men flew long distances, much of it over water (the 49th Fighter Group, with its P-40s, for example, was based at

Darwin in northern Australia), to engage in combat with superior Japanese aircraft, or to drop a small load of bombs without appreciable results. Planes that should have been junked were patched and flown until they fell apart. Some did, and airmen resented serving in a forgotten theater, forgotten because of the "Hitler first" strategy. Deliveries of supplies arrived slowly; and crates when they finally came, were found to have been pilfered by desperate crews en route. Disgruntled by poor food, miserable living conditions, and the methods of the Australian Air Force and its part in the operations, American airmen had grown apathetic and believed that if conditions prevailed, an Allied victory was hopeless.

The sacking of Brett would not solve all of the problems, but according to the workings of the military mind he was "responsible" (momentarily and conveniently excluding the Japanese) and therefore must go. And so it was that on August 4, 1942, stubby, cocky, pugnacious, and anything but aristocratic Major General George C. Kenney succeeded Brett as air commander in the Southwest Pacific. This tough, outspoken, practical, no-nonsense fighter found himself a rather lone figure in a nest of prima donnas and debilitated warriors.

Kenney, upon arriving in Brisbane, seat of MacArthur's command, was established in the air-conditioned Lennon's Hotel and spent some time listening to Sutherland berating the Australians, various American officers, with emphasis upon the consistently unlucky Lewis H. Brereton (who had been MacArthur's air commander in the Philippines), and, of course, the obstinate Brett. The Air Force was especially vile: ". . . none of Brett's staff or senior commanders was any good, the pilots didn't know much about flying, the bombers couldn't hit anything and knew nothing about proper maintenance of their equipment or how to handle their supplies. He also thought there was some question about the kids having much stomach for fighting. . . . In fact, I heard just about everyone hauled over the coals except Douglas MacArthur and Richard K. Sutherland."

Shrewdly the canny ex-World War I fighter pilot, whose experience with aircraft maintenance, production, and manipulation went back more than two decades, said little at this point. But he thought, ". . . Sutherland was inclined to overemphasize his [own] smattering of knowledge of aviation."

George Kenney, who ran the "air show" in Mac-Arthur's section of the Pacific. Down to earth, pragmatic, loyal, Kenney not only won over MacArthur but also his own men, whom he called "kids," because, in the main, that was what they were.

(U. S. AIR FORCE)

It was not until the next morning that Kenney was ushered in to meet with MacArthur, in lonely splendor, on the eighth floor of a nine-story office building in downtown Brisbane. After initial formalities, MacArthur began pacing and speaking, repeating the same criticisms of the Air Force which Sutherland had spouted the evening before. In MacArthur's view, "air personnel had gone beyond just being antagonistic to his headquarters, to the point of disloyalty. He would not stand for disloyalty."

During a pause in the outpouring of words, Kenney rose to full height (he was about a head shorter than MacArthur), deciding "it was time to lay my cards on the table."

He began by reminding MacArthur that he had come out to the Pacific because MacArthur had requested him and that "as long as he had had enough confidence in me to ask for me to be sent out to run his air show for him, I intended to do that very

B-17E, one of the few, based near Mareeba, Australia.
"A formation of five or six B-17s was regarded . . . as
. . . impressive . . ." (U. S. AIR FORCE)

thing." Kenney bluntly told the general that he could
run an "air show" better than or as well as anyone
available. The emphasis was on the fact that he—
Kenney—would run the air show. As for loyalty,
the day that Kenney no longer felt loyal to his chief,
"I would come and tell him so and at that time I
would be packed up and ready for the orders sending me back home."

MacArthur's stormy expression changed; the
fierce glint left his eyes. He studied the small man
before him, appraising him, then walked over, threw
an arm around Kenney's shoulders, and said,
"George, I think we are going to get along together
all right."

George Kenney served as air commander in the
Pacific from that day until the end of the war. If
he could pledge loyalty to MacArthur, whom he
genuinely admired, it was exceeded only by his de-
votion to his "kids," the young airmen who were
then fighting a great war with so little.

With characteristic promptitude, Kenney applied

himself to finding out what was wrong. He had
arrived on July 28 and would not assume command
until August 4. He found Brett's directorate system,
"with about a dozen people issuing orders in the
commander's name, . . . too complicated for me. I
decided to see how it worked first but I was afraid
I was not smart enough to figure it out. Further-
more, it looked to me as if there were too many
people in the headquarters. . . ."

In the interests of Allied co-operation, Kenney
found a rigid attempt to intermix Australian and
American throughout the organization. Obviously, it
did not always work. Despite the crowded office,
Kenney learned also that the bulk of the Allied
Air Staff, along with all personnel and supply rec-
ords, was based in Melbourne about eight hundred
miles distant. But not so distant as MacArthur, only
three floors above in the same building. Brett could
never reach the commander and was forced always
to deal through Sutherland. This was not Kenney's
way of running an air show.

That same evening he borrowed Brett's Flying
Fortress, the famed *Swoose,* which enjoyed a better
press than Brett and took off for the forward bases

in Australia and in New Guinea. At Port Moresby, in southern New Guinea, Kenney found little to comfort him. The organization and procedure were "chaotic." Bombing missions, for example, were assigned out of Brett's headquarters in Brisbane. Orders were then sent to Major General Ralph Royce in Townsville to the north; Royce, in turn, notified the 19th Bombardment Group (H), based at Mareeba, about two hundred miles north of Townsville, and "the 19th Group sent the number of airplanes it had in commission to Port Moresby, where they were refueled, given their final 'briefing' on weather conditions along the route to the target and whatever data had been picked up by air reconnaissance.

"The fighter group at Port Moresby [35th Fighter Group] sat around waiting for the Japs to come over and tried to get off the ground in time to intercept them, which they seldom did, as the warning service rarely gave the fighters over five minutes' notice that the Nip planes were on the way." Those aircraft which did get off the ground seemed to operate without leadership, even on bombing missions. A formation of five or six B-17s was regarded as an impressive number then in the Pacific, although what with problems with weather or engines, it was a good mission if three aircraft found the target—Japanese shipping or the bases at Rabaul. But the meager accomplishment rarely made the effort worth it. Kenney found, too, that aircrews frequently abandoned missions when Japanese aircraft intercepted them, fearing that a single bullet would detonate either the auxiliary fuel tanks or the bomb load. No one had thought to inform them that this was not necessarily true.

If MacArthur demanded that a man be loyal, Kenney insisted that he be an "operator." Within days after his arrival and inspection of conditions, quite a number of non-operators were sent back to the States. He found the system of supply especially reprehensible, overladen with an obsession with paper formality. "An average time of one month elapsed from the time the requisition started until it was returned, generally with the notation 'Not available' or 'Improperly filled out.'" When told that desperately needed replacement parts for combat aircraft were denied to the fighting units, Kenney found it difficult to believe, "but the kids made me eat my words when they showed me a whole filing case of returned requisition forms. I

took along a handful for future reference and as evidence that some of the people in the organization were playing on the wrong team."

Immediately, too, Kenney began sending in his own team of operators. He had discussed his views on the air situation in Australia and New Guinea with MacArthur, asking for authority to send anyone home he regarded as "deadwood." MacArthur concurred and Kenney moved quickly. He found men who were genuinely tired from earlier campaigns, or ill from Australian heat or New Guinea jungle; they deserved relief, but those "who were not pulling their weight could go home and the rest would move north to take their turns eating canned food and living in grass huts on the edge of the jungle."

Kenney had been preceded to the area by two competent officers, Brigadier Generals Kenneth N. Walker, a bombardment specialist, and Ennis C. Whitehead, a fighter commander. In time Walker would head Kenny's bomber command and Whitehead, as Kenney's deputy, moved into Port Moresby to command the advanced echelon of what was to become the Fifth Air Force. With him Kenney had brought young Major William Benn, who had served as his aide when Kenney was commander of the Fourth Air Force in San Francisco. Benn, as were Walker and Whitehead, was definitely an operator. Anxious to serve in a combat unit Benn was happy to be given command of the 63rd Squadron of the 43rd Bombardment Group, which at the time of Kenney's advent was depleted—"all they had left was a flag and a couple of guys to hold it up." As soon as the 43rd Group became operational with B-17s, it would take the work load off the much abused 19th Bomb Group, then commanded by Lieutenant Colonel Richard N. Carmichael. The 19th Group had been, in Kenney's words, "kicked out of the Philippines and out of Java and kicked around ever since."

Upon his arrival Kenney had requested an inventory of aircraft strength (when he had asked Brett, the latter told him simply that he did not know). According to the books, Kenney learned in a few days that he had "in the United States part of the show, 245 fighters, 53 light bombers, 70 medium bombers, 62 heavy bombers, 36 transports, and 51 miscellaneous aircraft, or a total of 517. ... The Australian Royal Air Force listed 22

An Airacobra and a B-17 nestled in revetments near Port Moresby, New Guinea. The P-39 was a disad- *vantaged contender as far as the Zero was concerned; the Fortress, the "E," with a stinger in the tail was respected by Japanese pilots.* (U. S. AIR FORCE)

squadrons, but most of these were equipped with training planes doing anti-submarine patrol off the coasts of Australia itself. Two fighter squadrons in New Guinea had a total of 40 planes, and four reconnaissance squadrons had a total of 30 aircraft."

But out of the 245 American fighters, 170 were awaiting salvage or were being overhauled, none of the light bombers were ready for operations, and "only 37 mediums were in shape or had guns and bomb racks to go to war with." Of the 62 heavy bombers only 43 were more or less fit to fly; less than half of the mixed bag of transports were flyable. As for the "miscellaneous" aircraft, none was fit for combat. A Dutch squadron, equipped with American B-25s, was training but required a good deal of time before it would be ready for combat.

"All told I had about 150 American and 70 Australian aircraft, scattered from Darwin to Port Moresby and back to Mareeba and Townsville, with which to dispute the air with the Jap." Kenney estimated that the Japanese had at least five times the number of planes he could muster, besides being in a position to replace losses within days from their homeland.

The greatest concentration of Japanese air power facing Kenney's forces was based at Rabaul, New Britain. The 25th Koku Sentai (Air Flotilla) consisting of the Tainan Kokutai (Air Corps), the 4th Kokutai, and the Yokohama Kokutai, under Rear Admiral Sadayoshi Yamada, operated from Rabaul chiefly against Port Moresby as well as Guadalcanal in the Solomons. These were land-based units, equipped with the Zero fighters; in addition there were bomber units (mediums: *Nell, Betty*) which attacked Port Moresby regularly and which gave occasional attention to Darwin and other Australian ports. In addition to the land-based planes there were also the planes of the Japanese carrier divisions to consider.

Until he could obtain better and more aircraft as well as replacements for tired crews, Kenney faced a formidable job.

By this time the Joint Chiefs of Staff had decided on a plan of operation giving priority to the Navy's proposal to move into the Solomons as against MacArthur's to move into New Guinea to seize and occupy the Buna area.

The honor, then, of making the first American offensive move in the Pacific fell to the U. S. Navy, not to MacArthur, under Vice-Admiral Robert L. Ghormley, commander of the South Pacific Area. The honor fell, more specifically and traditionally, to the 1st Marine Division, which was to assault the

Solomons. MacArthur's contribution to the offensive was to be a Kenney-mounted bombing mission against Rabaul. This small effort did not please MacArthur, nor did it comply with the image of himself as a major contributor to the offensive.

While these decisions were being made, the Japanese themselves began moving ashore at Buna on July 21, 1942. Having been thwarted in an invasion attempt at Port Moresby in the Battle of the Coral Sea, the Japanese hoped to move in on this chief Allied base by crossing over the Owen Stanley Mountains, through the Kokoda trail, to take Port Moresby from the rear. This would not only place Australia within more convenient striking distance, but would also serve as protection for Rabaul as well as the Solomons in the South Pacific.

The assault in the Solomons was scheduled for August 7, 1942, just about a week after Kenney had begun moving and shaking up his command. For his first official "show" he had promised MacAr-

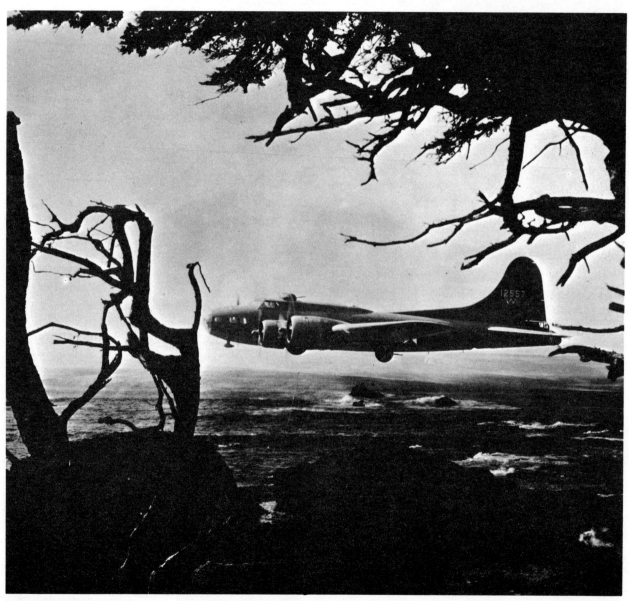

A Flying Fortress off the coast of New Guinea. About forty were operational when Kenney arrived to assume command of the air forces in the Southwest Pacific.

Zero pilots respected the big bomber, although many had been worn out by constant use.

(U. S. AIR FORCE)

thur that twenty B-17s would be ready for the mission and he guaranteed that sixteen to eighteen would bomb the target. MacArthur appeared skeptical, though hopefully commenting that, if so, it would be the "heaviest bomber concentration flown so far in the Pacific war."

One of Kenney's first moves upon visiting the base of the 19th Bombardment Group at Mareeba was to order all flying suspended until the group's B-17s could be put in some sort of flying condition. On the day of his visit Kenney found that a maximum effort by the group might have gotten about four bombers into the air. Engines were sadly worn and many planes were grounded for lack of tail wheels. Rather than bother with requisition forms, Kenney reached Major General Rush B. Lincoln, in Melbourne eight hundred miles distant, by phone and simply read off a list of the supplies required by Carmichael's group.

When he checked in at Mareeba a few days later, Kenney was gratified to hear that Carmichael hoped to have twenty B-17s ready for the mission to Rabaul. So great a number of aircraft caused some concern among squadron commanders when Kenney impressed them with the importance of holding formation—they had not flown in such large numbers before. Defensive formations were important to the bombers to hold off, with their gun concentrations, attacking Japanese fighters.

On the morning of August 7, 1942, Carmichael had sixteen B-17s at Port Moresby, where they refueled after flying up from Mareeba. While the Marines were heading in for their objectives in the Solomons—Tulagi, Gavutu, Tanambogo, and Guadalcanal—Carmichael led his formation over the treacherous Owen Stanleys to Rabaul. There were now thirteen B-17s; one having crashed on takeoff and two others having been forced back with engine trouble. Proceeding on to Rabaul and the bomber base, Vunakanau, the Fortresses encountered fighters, little dancing Zeros which swarmed in around the bombers. During the attacks one Fortress, piloted by Captain Harl Pease (whose aircraft was not functioning properly) was shot down burning; it was the only B-17 lost in the attack. Bombs pirouetted down upon the parked bombers of Vunakanau, wreaking havoc and leaving smoking bombers to clutter the runway. Kenney thought eleven of the twenty Japanese fighters were de-

stroyed, but another claim amounted to seven. Whatever the claims, Japanese fighters and bombers of Rabaul had been kept busy during the Solomons landings. Kenney was also certain that the bombing had destroyed perhaps seventy-five parked aircraft, although the figure appears rather generous. Some fighters of the Tainan Kokutai had rushed down to Guadalcanal to challenge Marine and Navy fighter planes over the invasion beaches. In this battle Japanese ace Saburo Sakai accounted for four American planes before being seriously wounded himself and his Zero shot up. All but blinded by his wounds, Sakai managed to fly his damaged plane over the nearly six hundred miles from Guadalcanal back to Rabaul.

The success, though limited, of the 19th Group's Rabaul mission was good for the group's morale and for Kenney's reputation as an "operator." He quickly revealed a near-fiendish inventiveness in dealing with the air situation in the Pacific. Soon (by August 9) he could announce the formation of the Fifth Air Force and began injecting spirit into it and developing its personality in his own aggressive image.

II

Kenney, as he explained to MacArthur, visualized his primary mission as the taking out of Japanese air power "until we owned the air over New Guinea. There was no use talking about playing across the street until we got the Nips off of our front lawn."

His methods were far from conventional. During his flight from the United States to Australia, Kenney had discussed with his aide, Major William Benn, the possibilities of low-altitude bombing to knock out ships. This was not, in fact, a new concept. Earlier in the summer Benn had observed demonstrations of the idea at the Eglin Field, Florida, proving ground. Here the hope of bouncing bombs into tanks from fighters was being tested under the direction of Colonel Sargent Huff. The British had also tried minimal-altitude bombing, but had given it up. It remained for Kenney and Benn to give the idea its special significance in the Pacific. High-altitude bombing, such as had been attempted at Midway by the B-17s, proved ineffective. Since the Japanese were dependent upon "open-water defense" (that is, shipping supplies and reinforcements to their outposts in large convoys), thus counting upon the vastness of the Pacific, the ability of ships to maneuver, and their own Navy and aircraft to protect them, dealing with ships at sea presented a challenge. As they flew eastward, Kenney and Benn considered the possibilities of swooping down close to the water, much like a Navy torpedo bomber, to eject the bomb from the plane. Dropped at the correct speed, altitude (about mast-high), and distance from the ship, the bomb with delayed-action fuzes literally skipped along the water until it struck the side of the vessel. It would then, ideally, sink a little and detonate against the side of the ship. Meanwhile, the bomber would have cleared the enemy ship and hurtled away from the scene of the explosion. Shortly after their arrival in Australia, Kenney "fired" Benn as his aide and placed him in command of the 63rd Squadron (43rd Bombardment Group) so that he might test the feasibility of "skip-bombing" with the B-17.

Kenny realized that in order for his skip-bomber to be effective it must be able to overwhelm the deck defenses of Japanese ships. The skip-bomber must have plenty of firepower in the nose, a problem he turned over to a slender, tanned, raffish character, Major Paul I. Gunn. Because he was over forty, Gunn was nicknamed "Pappy" by the younger pilots and was so called even by Kenney, himself then about fifty.

When the war began in 1941, Gunn was an experienced pilot and operations manager of the new Philippine Air Lines. As a captain the second day of the war Gunn began a legendary career flying supplies, evacuating refugees, and accomplishing impossible flying feats under the eyes and guns of the Japanese. He used the Philippine Air Lines civilian Beechcrafts for his missions, frequently hugging the ground and thinking how much harm he could do to the Japanese if only he had had guns installed in the nose of the Beechcraft. This was not, of course, an original conception, for the concept of attack aviation was not in itself new (Kenney, in fact, had taught the subject in the Air Corps Tactical School for a decade). One of the Air Force units Kenney found languishing in Australia when he arrived was the 3rd Bombardment Group (Light), specialists in ground assault and equipped with the Douglas A-24 (Dauntless), the Douglas

A-20 (Havoc), and a third squadron with the North American B-25; the fourth squadron had no planes at all.

The "fortunes of war" brought together Kenney, Benn and his skip-bombing Flying Fortresses, the 3rd Group's assortment of twin-engined attack planes, and the wild-flying, resourceful Pappy Gunn.

If MacArthur had a historic mission to fulfill in his promise to return to the Philippines, Gunn had a deeper, more personal one. When the air forces were scrambled out of the Philippines after the fall of Corregidor in May of 1942, Gunn's wife and four children were imprisoned at the Santo Tomás prison camp near Manila.

Walter D. Edmonds perceptively observed ". . . Pappy Gunn governed himself as though there were two wars against Japan: the one the United States had on its hands, and his own. He fought them both."

Kenney had one other device in mind when he arrived to take over the Allied Air Forces in the Southwest Pacific. "Back in 1928," Kenney has written, "in order to drop bombs in a low-altitude attack without having the fragments hit the airplane I had put parachutes on the bombs; the parachutes opened as the bombs were released from the airplane. . . . With a supersensitive fuze, which kicked the thing off instantaneously on contact with anything—even the leaf of a bush—the bomb was a wicked little weapon. . . ." These so-called "parafrags" were small bombs, weighing about twenty-five pounds, which fragmented in more than a thousand pieces that could "go through a two-inch plank." Kenney's targets were not planks, of course, and he considered "trying them out on some Jap airdrome and wondering if those fragments would tear airplanes apart—as well as Japs, too, if they didn't get out of the way." It was while he was in Washington awaiting transportation to the Pacific and "looking around for anything that was not nailed down" that Kenney found several thousand of his parachute bombs still stored away. He had them shipped to Australia.

Another wicked weapon was named the "Kenney Cocktail"; this was a standard M-47 100-pound bomb loaded with white phosphorus which, when it burst, flung out streamers of burning incendiary material in all directions for 150 feet. Its effect upon man and machine was deadly. By the end of

A Douglas A-20 "Havoc" demonstrating a skip-bombing on a Japanese freighter. Splashes to left of ship mark the spots at which the bombs bounced (two from the photo ship and two from the Havoc in the photograph). One of the dangers of skip-bombing was collision with the target; another was being caught in your own bomb explosion. This type of bombing required great skill. (U. S. AIR FORCE)

1942 Kenney's name was known in Tokyo whose radio referred to him as "the Beast" and one of the "gangster leaders of a gang of gangsters from a gangster-ridden country."

Kenney held no grand strategic illusions. He wished "to own the air over New Guinea" primarily so that MacArthur's ground troops, Australian and later American, could push the Japanese over the Owen Stanley Mountains back to Buna and out of New Guinea. Co-operation with the ground forces would be essential to this design. "Tanks and heavy artillery can be reserved for the battlefields of Europe and Africa," Kenney wrote to his chief, Arnold. "They have no place in jungle warfare. The artillery in this theater flies. . . .

"In the Pacific theater we have a number of islands garrisoned by small forces. These islands are nothing more or less than aerodromes or aerodrome areas from which modern fire-power is launched."

"The Air Force is the spearhead of the Allied attack in the Southwest Pacific," Kenney believed. "Its function is to clear the air, wreck the enemy's land installations, destroy his supply system, and give close support to troops advancing on the ground.

"Clearing the air means more than air superiority; it means air control so supreme that the birds have to wear our Air Force insignia. Wrecking the enemy's ground installations does not mean just softening them up. It means taking out everything he has —aerodromes, guns, bunkers, troops. Destroying his supply system means cutting him off the vine so completely and firmly that he not only cannot undertake offensive action but, due to his inability to replenish his means to wage war, he cannot even maintain a successful defense."

In order to carry out his mission, however, Kenney was forced to improvise and get along as best he could with what little he had. One of the innovations was a converted Havoc (A-20 light bomber), the handiwork of Pappy Gunn, which instead of its meager four .30-caliber machine guns had an additional four .50 calibers in the nose. Its limited range, too, had been increased with the introduction of two 450-gallon fuel tanks in the bomb bay which would give the Havoc the additional fuel to get over the 13,000-foot barrier of the Owen Stanleys. One further modification was a fanciful bomb rack installed in the old bomb bay; this carried the parachute-fragmentation bombs which Kenney wished to try out on a Japanese airfield.

The first opportunity arrived on September 12, 1942. Captain Donald P. Hall led nine Havocs of the 89th Attack Squadron (of the 3rd Bombardment Group) in low over the Buna, New Guinea, airstrip. The first element, with Hall in the van, swooped in over the palm trees and saw to their delight a number of new enemy aircraft neatly lined up on the strip. With their forward firing guns churning up the area before them the Havocs swept over the Buna strip scattering parafrags (forty per plane) in their wake. As the light bombs gently lowered to the ground aroused Japanese guards, apparently assuming paratroopers were being dropped, rushed out to fire at them. Until the first supersensitive fuze touched something, the hapless riflemen did not realize how exposed they were to the vicious effect of the descending silken packages.

The primary objective was, however, aircraft, and Hall's bombers scattered the bombs across the airstrip and pulled away to escape the bomb blasts— as well as Japanese antiaircraft fire. The parafrags, falling about fifty yards apart, began doing their work, wrecking aircraft (claims were made for sev-

enteen of the twenty-two planes on the strip) and very quickly discouraging both the men with rifles and the antiaircraft crews. The second wave strung out its bombs with no interference from the ground. To complete the job, postholing the airstrip itself, Kenney followed the Havoc attack with B-26s and B-17s (five of the former, seven of the latter), which bombed from higher up with thousand-pounders onto the runways. Not one American plane was lost and the first parafrag mission was judged a success, for even if the claims for aircraft destroyed were exaggerated, serious damage had been done at Buna.

By this time the Japanese were dangerously near Port Moresby, pushing the Australian 7th Division before them. Upon seeing the situation firsthand, Kenney flew back to Australia, suggesting that the Australians be reinforced with Americans of the 32nd Division. Although MacArthur felt the 32nd was ill trained, he realized that unless the Japanese were stopped before reaching Moresby, Australia itself would become a battleground. He had decided to send the 32nd Division to New Guinea and put his staff to work arranging for transportation.

Kenney suggested flying the troops to Port Moresby; MacArthur's eyes lit up, but his staff demurred. After all, when a body of water intervened between the place where you wished to send troops and the place where they were at, it followed that you placed these troops on ships for transport. This was the normal way to do it. It would also take two weeks, Kenney argued. Planes would get them there in a day or two. To MacArthur's staff this just didn't seem proper and they wanted the movement to proceed "in an orderly way." But MacArthur elected to let Kenney fly the 126th Regiment of the 32nd into Moresby. By borrowing transport planes from the Australians Kenney transported the first 230 infantrymen to Port Moresby by the evening of September 15, 1942; the rest of the regiment was still waiting at the docks. Disappointed, Kenney asked to be given another regiment (the 128th Infantry), and over the protests of his staff MacArthur said all right.

Soon ground troops were arriving in Port Moresby at a rate of six hundred a day. By this time Kenney was using a dozen Australian civil transports and even had American civilians working for him. Two B-17s had arrived from the United States with ci-

Factory-fresh Lockheed P-38 "Lightning," which relieved the P-40 and P-39 in the Pacific. No dogfighter, *it was heavy and sturdy and carried plenty of firepower. Its twin engines were an added safety device.*
(ERIK MILLER/LOCKHEED-CALIFORNIA)

vilian pilots, employees of the Boeing Company. Kenney pressed them into service and soon the B-17s were ferrying troops out of Australia. The last of the 128th Infantry had been transported to Port Moresby and the remainder of the 126th Infantry was still at sea; they arrived two days later. MacArthur was elated, Kenney was "crowing," and MacArthur's staff was put out. There were dark suggestions voiced within MacArthur's hearing that Kenney was "reckless and irresponsible."

Kenney's job did not conclude with the delivery of the bulk of the 32nd Division to Port Moresby. He would have to see that they were supplied, that various Japanese airfields—Rabaul, Lae in New Guinea—were given attention, besides bombing and strafing Japanese emplacements along the Kokoda trail. Further, there were calls for assistance in the South Pacific from Admiral Ghormley and the Solomons campaign. This generally called for B-17s to bomb Rabaul during the day and Catalinas of the Royal Australian Air Force during the night.

III

The Japanese too had the problem of supply and replacement. Like MacArthur's staff, their thinking favored the "orderly way," which generally meant large convoys of ships, transports with escorts. Supply by air, though not completely ignored, was not seriously considered by the Japanese. Once the air over New Guinea was owned by Kenney, it left the Japanese convoys open to aerial attack. By the end of the year Kenney had acquired some B-24s (this was the 90th Bombardment Group), which were plagued, however with mechanical problems (cracked nosewheel collars) and out of action for a month. When new collars were specially manufactured and the group made its first missions in mid-November 1942, it demonstrated a need for further training (on the second mission—to Rabaul—the B-24 carrying Group Commander Colonel Arthur Meehan did not return, nor did one other, and the other crews had little idea of where they had been). This was a bitter development for Kenney, who had already relieved the overworked 19th Bombardment Group, which had begun flying their equally overworked B-17s back to the United States. In

time, however, the 90th Bombardment Group's B-24s—and crews—were ready. They would then join up with Kenney's then only active heavy group, the 43rd.

Also arriving in the Pacific by the end of 1942 was the Lockheed P-38 ("Lightning"), a plane which seemed unloved in Europe, but which Kenney favored for the simple reason that it flew. There were other good reasons, of course, once the kinks were ironed out of the plane (initially leakage in the intercooling system); it was a superb fighter for the Pacific theater. Its twin engines was one of its blessings, considering the distances over which it must range. A single-engined craft simply went down and out, but with its two engines, the P-38 could lose one and still return to its base. It was a great, heavy aircraft for a fighter and although it could not match the Zero in dogfighting, it proved to be the scourge of the Japanese fighter in the Pacific. The Lightning was faster than the Zero, achieving a top speed of more than four hundred miles an hour; it could outclimb and outdive the Japanese fighter, performed exceptionally well at high altitude, and carried plenty of firepower (20-mm. cannon and four .50-caliber machine guns). In addition, the P-38 came equipped with features which the Japanese hardly considered (because they added weight): self-sealing fuel tanks and armor plating to protect the pilot.

Twenty-five Lightnings had arrived in Brisbane in September but remained grounded until the various mechanical defects had been cleared up. Newly arrived pilots were forced to wait until the P-38s were ready or use the worn-out P-39s and P-40s for combat. The bugs were not eliminated from the P-38s until December; meanwhile another batch of twenty-five arrived but without feeds for the guns —these too were grounded until the feeds could be installed. Finally, by October Kenney had sixteen P-38s of the 49th Fighter Group flown up to Port Moresby. Further complications set in what with leakages discovered in the cooling system, problems with disintegrating wing tanks—and "borrowing" of the operational P-38s by the South Pacific command for the Solomons campaign.

Eventually, in December 1942, the P-38s began to operate. The first Japanese plane brought down by one was achieved in an unorthodox manner. According to General Kenney "a big good-natured New Orleans Cajun named Faurot" was flying over

Japanese fighter pilots, who "owned the air" over New Guinea when Kenney arrived to take over the aerial operations for MacArthur. These Zero pilots, often victorious over American and Australian pilots in their P-40s and P-39s, would find the arrival of the Lightning in the Pacific a serious challenge to their superiority. (DEFENSE DEPT., U. S. MARINE CORPS)

the Japanese air base at Lae. For days the Americans had radioed insulting messages (Japanese and Americans exchanged such insults over their radios in English), but without inciting the Zeros to come up. Faurot on this day carried, as did the others in the flight, two five-hundred-pound bombs under his plane's wing. The plan was to make holes in the runway at Lae. Finally after the by now traditional exchange of insults the Americans had succeeded in arousing one of the Japanese pilots. His Zero had begun a takeoff run when Faurot noticed him and dived. He was down to two thousand feet when he recalled that he carried a thousand pounds of bomb, which would deter him immeasurably if he and the Zero tangled. Faurot quickly released the two five-hundred-pounders, pulled back on the control column to escape the blast, and pulled around in a turn, ready to pounce on the Zero. As he watched, the two bombs fell into the water at the end of the runway, which ran right to the beach. The resultant splash caught the Japanese plane, at that moment at runway's end and lifting off the ground. The Zero lurched crazily and careened into the water, a total wreck.

"When the kids returned, I asked Faurot if he had nerve enough to claim 'the first Nip brought down in air combat in this theater by a P-38.' He grinned and asked if I was going to give him an Air Medal. I had promised one to anyone that got an official victory. I said, 'Hell, no. I want you to shoot them down, not splash water on them.'" Kenney, whose relationship with his "kids" was marked by an affectionate, bantering humor of the crusty father, awarded Faurot his Air Medal, although warning him that "he'd better keep the whole thing quiet."

With a few airplanes to his credit and some new eager kids to fly them, Kenney felt himself reasonable able to take on the "Nip" in his own back yard. Curiously this was echoed, almost in Kenney's own words, in a Japanese diary found in New Guinea. Early in December 1942 the diarist noted of Kenney's Kids that "they fly above our position as if they owned the skies."

Kenney's first great opportunity to prove himself in a spectacular manner came in March 1943. Buna on the northeast coast of New Guinea was wrested from the Japanese—after a half year of savage ground fighting—in January; Guadalcanal, in the Solomons, had been reluctantly abandoned by the Japanese, also following a half year of sanguinary land, sea, and air battles leading to the first major land defeat by the Japanese. The Nipponese tenta-

Lightning in battle dress showing its armament: a 20-mm. cannon and three of the four .50-caliber machine guns in the nose. (ERIK MILLER/LOCKHEED-CALIFORNIA)

cles into the Solomons and New Guinea constricted bloodily. In the Solomons the focus shifted to the northernmost island, Bougainville; in New Guinea it moved up the coast, about 150 miles from Buna to the Lae-Salamaua area in the Huon Gulf.

Having abandoned Guadalcanal and Buna the Japanese proceeded to reinforce their position at Lae. Late in February 1943 Kenney's intelligence unit had learned that a Japanese convoy, forming at Rabaul, was scheduled to arrive in Lae early in March. This would coincide with a period of bad weather predicted for the area, which would curtail air operations. Although the information was meager, Kenney sensed a large-scale troop movement in the offing. He alerted General Whitehead at Port Moresby and ordered reconnaissance aircraft to cover the area of the Bismarck Sea.

Meanwhile about five thousand troops of the Japanese 51st Infantry Division assigned to reinforce the Lae-Salamaua garrison had begun boarding seven merchant vessels in Rabaul Harbor. Eight destroyers were to serve as escort, along with an air cover of about a hundred fighters (not simultaneously, but on a schedule in order to furnish protection over a period of days, generally in groups of twenty to thirty). Special service vessel *Nojima* rounded out the convoy of sixteen ships; aboard one of the transports, the *Kembu Maru,* besides troops, was a precious cargo of aviation fuel and other supplies.

The convoy set forth under cover of darkness and stormy weather the night of February 28. The weather hindered Kenney's reconnaissance planes and it was not until the afternoon of March 1 that a B-24 crew spotted "fourteen ships with Zero escort" about 150 miles west of Rabaul. The weather closed in again, preventing further spotting as well as an attack by eight B-17s of the 43rd Group which did not locate the convoy.

The weather continued bad on March 2 and it took until midmorning before a 90th Group B-24 found the convoy and radioed its position—about fifty miles north of Cape Gloucester, New Britain, heading south for the Vitiaz Straits. As soon as possible the 43rd Group's B-17s left Port Moresby, climbed the Owen Stanleys, and began dropping thousand-pound bombs from sixty-five hundred feet. This first flight of eight Flying Fortresses made the attack without fighter protection, having missed its

rendezvous with the P-38s. Zeros closed in and in the fighting three were claimed shot down; all B-17s returned to Port Moresby claiming hits on two transports, reporting that one had split in two and sank within minutes of the initiation of the attack. This was the *Kyokusei Maru,* whose survivors, about eight hundred men, were taken aboard two destroyers and rushed to Lae during the night. The destroyers rejoined the convoy early the next morning.

A second flight of B-17s, twenty in all, followed the first to continue the bombing, claiming two hits and several near misses. Crews reported ships dead in the war, burning or sinking as well as the rescue operations of the two Japanese destroyers. Further defensive attacks by Zeros holed the B-17s but did not knock any of the bombers down; one Zero was claimed. In the early evening further bombing attacks by the 43rd Group near the northern entrance to the Vitiaz Straits claimed one vessel "left sinking" and another Zero. Enemy fighters, it was noted, were less persistent than in the earlier phases of the battle. As the sudden tropical night fell, the B-17s returned to Port Moresby while a Royal Australian Air Force PBY Catalina remained over the Japanese convoy during the night; in the morning a B-17 appeared to relieve the Catalina and found the convoy off the Huon Peninsula and within striking range of the medium bombers.

On Wednesday, March 3 at "ten o'clock the big brawl began about 50 miles southeast of Finschhafen, right where we had planned it," Kenney has written. Australian Beauforts of the RAAF 9th Operational Group carrying torpedoes opened the attack but without success; soon after, Australian Beaufighters, armed with nose cannons and machine guns in the wings, swooped in for a low-level attack. Above the Beaufighters B-17s co-ordinated a high-altitude attack and B-25s a medium-level attack with the Beaufighters. The sea churned with the explosion of bombs, the splash of cannon, and machine-gun fire whipping across the dodging Japanese ships. Thousands of feet above the carnage Zeros and P-38s fought their battles. The Battle of the Bismarck Sea had reached a climax.

Following the Beaufighter, B-17, and B-25 attack, twelve B-25Cls, newly converted into powerful strafers by the hand of Pappy Gunn and led by Major Edward Larner of the 90th Squadron (3rd

*A direct hit upon a Japanese ship in the Bismarck
Sea. The wake of the evasive circle of the ship may
be seen.* (U. S. AIR FORCE)

Bombardment Group), swept down to the water
for the most savage attack of the battle.

Larner was one of Kenney's favorites among his
kids. When Kenney first met Larner the latter was a
lieutenant who had "fire, leadership, and guts." This
had been demonstrated during the Buna campaign
at least twice, the first time during a strafing run
on Japanese artillery and machine-gun positions at
Soputa, just inland from Buna. Larner, leading the
90th Squadron, blazed in on the gun positions at a
low level. An antiaircraft burst under the tail of his
plane, tipping its nose, flung Larner's plane through
the treetops for hundreds of yards, battering the
plane as well as various trees. As laconically reported by the pilot, "following this accident I was
able to make only two more strafing passes before
the plane became so unmanageable that I thought
it best to return to base where repairs could be
made."

As Kenney observed, Larner landed the B-25 at
nearly 175 miles an hour because of the damages
to the wing surfaces which affected the lift. The
underside of the plane was grooved where a palm
tree had grazed it; the wing was dented and gouged

*Battle of the Bismarck Sea: Japanese destroyer in
distress, burning, losing oil, and dead in the water
after Kenney's Fifth Air Force bombers hit it.*

(U. S. AIR FORCE)

and one engine was stuffed with foliage and bits of branches. The plane was in a condition that would have normally suggested abandonment, but Larner brought it home instead. Kenney gave him a Silver Star and promoted him to captain.

The second incident occurred when Larner brought his B-25 down low to strafe a Japanese machine-gun position—so low that the aircraft's tail bumper had hit the ground and dragged through the sand for several yards. Larner explained that he had been forced to go so low because he had "to look in the windows of the bunker to see what to shoot at."

As he studied the scraped-up plane, Kenney stood with one of Larner's machine gunners. The sergeant sighed audibly and said, "I guess I'll have to quit this pilot of mine. He's gone nuts. He runs into trees and tears 'em down and now he thinks he's a farmer and he's started plowing up the ground with his tail bumper. . . ."

Catching the mood, Kenney replied with the suggestion that he could fix it up. "I've got a chauffeur over at my headquarters who wants to shoot a pair of fifty-caliber guns. How about swapping jobs?"

The gunner hesitated just an instant before answering. "General I'd better stick. You see, Captain Larner is so crazy he really needs me to look after him."

So it was that Major Larner lead his strafers down into the melee that had become the Battle of the Bismarck Sea. The twelve B-25s, each with eight forward-firing .50-caliber machine guns in the nose, plus two in the top turret—ten in all—razed all before them as they came in at five hundred feet. The Japanese ships broke convoy formation and scrambled in an attempt to get out of the way. The B-25s swirled and separated, selecting a target. Waiting in an 89th Squadron Havoc, Pilot Edward Chudoba heard the B-25 pilots arguing over targets as the radio sputtered, "This is my ship—go get yourself a ship!"

The machine-gun fire blasted the decks clear of return fire as Larner's squadron bore down upon the dodging Japanese ships. At the correct point of release, five-hundred-pound bombs were flung from the B-25s and skipped along the water. Of the thirty-seven released the 90th Squadron claimed seventeen as direct hits. The destroyer *Arashio* took three of them, snapped out of control, and smashed into the

already hit *Nojima*. The *Nojima* sank within minutes and the *Arashio* sank several hours later. This meant that its crew was to suffer the further attentions from the planes which followed.

Having caused frightful distress to the convoy (a cruiser and a transport sank, two destroyers and seven other ships were damaged), Larner led his B-25s back to Port Moresby. All twelve of his planes returned, although one, shot up in the attack, crashed during its landing run without serious injury to the crew.

The 89th Squadron, also of the 3rd Bombardment Group, followed the 90th, in their Havocs. "I got my first sight of the battle," Edward Chudoba later recalled, "when a ship ahead and to the left blew up, throwing flames a half mile into the air. I thought it was a destroyer, but the destroyer I had marked in that position slowly pulled away revealing a tanker [this may have been the *Kembu Maru* with its cargo of men, replacement parts, and aviation fuel] beyond it sending up flames and smoke from stem to stern. . . .

One of "Pappy" Gunn's "commerce destroyers," a B-25 with four .50-caliber machine guns in the nose and two on either side of the fuselage just below the wing. The bombardier's compartment was removed and so was the Mitchell's lower turret. The eight forward-firing guns concentrated a withering fire in the plane's path. (U. S. AIR FORCE)

"We were now about opposite the middle of the convoy on its port [left] side. Our two Vs of six Havocs each wheeled almost at right angles to the left to come in against it broadside. We were sliding down from about 2,000 feet now at an angle that would have us brushing the masts as we went over the enemy ships. . . .

"The time was exactly 10:03. The ships ahead were rapidly growing larger now.

"Young Charles Mayo (just turned twenty-one), my right wingman, and I were flying on the right side of our V of six ships. There was a ship ahead and two to the left. I dived and turned to the left under Captain Clark, our flight leader, and Mayo followed me. But the two planes on the left side of our V formation were going after the nearest ship on the left. I swung back and toward the big ship ahead. In spite of Captain Clark's warning not to pile up on the same ship, things were getting a bit confusing. I looked over my shoulder and there was Clark behind me. Young Mayo on my right said, 'I'm going off and get me a fat one.'

"The ship was rushing broadside at me now. I pulled the trigger on the wheel that started my machine guns spurting. I could see tracers and big stuff coming from the ship. I was pulling the bomb switch when a bullet came through the plexiglass canopy. Thirty caliber, I found later. I couldn't see a man on deck. The gun crews were well hidden. I let my two 500-pound bombs go now, just as I used to release them on calm days to skip against that old wreck at Port Moresby.

"Wham! I got it just as I passed over the ship. Ol' *Adam LaZonga* shuddered with the blow. (The plane was named for the great lover of the Li'l Abner strip and *Adam* sure could take it.) There was something wrong with the right wing and the plane wasn't flying right. I thought I had been hit with ack-ack. Captain Clark told me later that I had clipped off the top of the ship's radio mast. There was a dent on the front surface of my wing six inches deep."

The target was one of the troop-carrying transports, the *Tamei Maru,* which sank. All twelve of the 89th Squadron's Havocs returned to Port Moresby. During the battle Chudoba overheard radio conversations between the bombers and fighters, for the Zeros had begun concentrating on the B-17s in this climactic phase of the battle.

"Hey, Joe," Chudoba heard a Fortress pilot yell, "come on down. I've got three Zeros on my tail."

"Come on up," Joe said. "I have thirty of them."

The thirty or so Zero pilots must have been hard pressed to make any decision as to which planes to attack: the skip-bombing Mitchells and Havocs, the Beaufighters below, the B-25s in between, or the B-17s above. The Fortresses were the largest and appeared therefore to be the deadliest, so many Zeros attempted to get at them. One flown by Lieutenant Woodrow W. Moore was severely hit in the wing, which burst into flame. Moore ordered the bombs salvoed and the crew to jump. Seven managed to get out of the plane before it went into a steep dive and plunged into the Pacific, taking Moore with it.

As the seven chutes floated down the Zeros strafed them. Captain Robert Faurot (he who had splashed down the first Japanese plane with a P-38) left the fighting and with his two wingmen, Lieutenants Hoyt A. Eason and Fred D. Schifflet, all of the 35th Fighter Group, dived down to aid the helpless bomber crewmen. All ten men, the seven in parachutes as well as the fighter pilots, perished in the ensuing fight, although Kenney believed that the P-38 pilots took "five Japs along with them."

These four aircraft, one B-17 and three P-38s, were the only Allied planes lost in the Battle of the Bismarck Sea. Although the weather turned sour by the afternoon of March 3, a few more strikes were made by B-17s, Larner's B-25s again and RAAF Bostons of the 9th Operational Group. It was the final co-ordinated attack, for the battle was over except for such details as mopping up, sinking ships that remained above water but could not move, and picking up survivors, if any.

Five torpedo boats of the U. S. Navy's Seventh Fleet (*"MacArthur's Navy"*) slipped into the battle area after dark that night and sank one of the crippled ships, and on the morning of the next day, Thursday, March 4, bombers dispatched another stray. The battle was as good as over and high jubilation ensued in the Fifth Air Force. Kenney, about to leave for conferences in Washington, wired Whitehead: *Congratulations on that stupendous success. Air Power has written some important history in the past three days. Tell the whole gang that I am so proud of them I am about to blow a fuze.*

Historian Samuel Eliot Morison, with exceptional grace for a Navy man, called the Battle of the Bismarck Sea "the most devastating air attack on ships of the entire war, excepting only that on Pearl Harbor." At the cost of thirteen men killed, twelve wounded, and four aircraft (plus two which crash-landed), Kenney's forces had sunk every transport (probably eight, although exact figures seem never to have been determined) and four destroyers for a total of twelve of the original eighteen ships which had left Rabaul. An estimated three thousand Japanese troops went down with the transports, about half of those which had boarded the ships; of the six thousand troops intended for Lae only about eight hundred reached there. These were the survivors of the sinking of the *Kyokusei Maru,* which the B-17s had broken in half in the initial attack of the battle on March 2.

For the Japanese it was almost as shocking a defeat as Midway. But in addition to the loss of men, ships, and aircraft (claims were made for twenty), it meant something even more costly: the end of large-scale supply and reinforcement runs to northeastern New Guinea. The beleaguered Japanese troops must subsist from that day on on what little could be brought in by barge, submarine, and other small craft.

The ultimate effect upon the development of the situation in New Guinea was far-reaching indeed. It meant that MacArthur could seriously consider moving up the carapace of the turtle-shaped island and toward the Philippines.

2

"CLEARING THE AIR"

THE Battle of the Bismarck Sea had been unique; the Japanese would never again place so many men and ships within the range of land-based aircraft. But if the sea was less a threat, there still remained along the line of MacArthur's projected advance in New Guinea several Japanese air bases at Lae (including those at nearby Salamaua and Nadzab) and at Wewak (a complex of fields including those at But, Dagua, and Boram). At the same time there was also the target at Rabaul, New Britain, with its inviting Simpson Harbour and several air bases: Vunakanau, Keravat, Lakunai, Rapopo, and Tobera. From Rabaul the Japanese were capable of interfering with MacArthur's plans in New Guinea as well as those of Vice-Admiral William F. Halsey (who had relieved Ghormley as commander) in the South Pacific.

Kenney therefore unleashed the devastating fury of his Pappy Gunn gadgetry upon Japanese shipping and air power along the route of the proposed Allied advance. He hoped to "clear the air" with everything he had until the Japanese had nothing.

With the Buna area secured, it was possible to establish airstrips at nearby Dobodura; thus the fighters, especially, were spared the high haul over the Owen Stanleys. MacArthur had his strategic eye next upon the Huon Peninsula, particularly Lae and Salamaua. But these targets lay nearly two hundred miles west of Dobodura, which meant that although within fighter range, the time possible over the target was so brief for the fighters that they could give little protection to the bombers. Consequently, Kenney sent out Lieutenant Everette E. Frazier, an aviation engineer attached to the Fifth Air Force, to scout out the location for an advance airdrome within flying distance of Lae and the Wewak complex of Japanese airdromes.

Frazier, by air and by foot in the jungle, covered hundreds of square miles of New Guinea until he found a likely spot, all but under the very noses of the Japanese in the vicinity of Marilinan, more specifically at the village of Tsili-Tsili, within sixty miles of the Japanese at Lae. Kenney preferred calling the location Marilinan—"it was a pretty name" —in case "the Nips should take us out, somebody might throw that Tsili-Tsili thing back at me." While the base was being built Kenney decoyed the Japanese to another position, which was made to look like an active installation. The Japanese bombed the decoy spot and somehow did not find the Marilinan base until it was completed and operating. By mid-August more than three thousand troops were based in the area, including the 2nd Air Task Force, commanded by Lieutenant Colonel Malcolm A. Moore and later by Colonel David W. Hutchison.

The Japanese bombed the forward base for the first time on August 15, 1943, when a dozen Sallys escorted by a dozen Zeros swooped down by sur-

A C-47 (the civilian Douglas DC-3) of the 6th Troop Carrier Squadron, with P-39 escort, flying over New Guinea. (U. S. AIR FORCE)

amounted to one Thunderbolt. After these two costly attempts, the Japanese chose to leave Marilinan reasonably unmolested.

On the next day, August 17, 1943, Kenney opened up his campaign upon the Wewak airdromes. Reconnaissance photos revealed more than two hundred aircraft distributed among the installations at But, Boram, Dagua, and Wewak. It was after midnight that B-17s and B-24s from Port Moresby began dropping bombs on the various targets. Although Japanese night fighters attempted interception, antiaircraft fire and searchlights proved to be the most formidable, resulting in the loss of three heavy bombers. Early morning photographs accounted for "at least 18 unserviceable" aircraft left on the Japanese airdromes, in addition to the damage to the strips which two hundred tons of bombs could do. But this was only the curtain raiser designed to foul the strips in order to interfere with Japanese aerial efforts during the next act.

At dawn the B-25 "Strafers," with P-38 escort, slashed across the tops of the palm trees in the Wewak area for the climax of "the show." Lieutenant Colonel Donald P. Hall, who had first experimented with the parafrag bomb during the early days of the Buna campaign, led the 8th and 13th Squadrons (3rd Bombardment Group) down upon the strips at Boram. It was, as Kenney observed, a "sight to gladden the heart of a strafer." Japanese bombers, perhaps sixty or more, lined up on both sides of the runway with engines warming up in preparation for

prise and shot down a C-47 carrying men of the ground echelons of the 35th Fighter Group, stationed at Marilinan; another transport crashed into the jungle and was never found. Escorting P-39s tangled with the bombers and fighters while the other C-47s sought refuge in the treetops and flew back to the comparative safety of Port Moresby. Four P-39s (but only one pilot) were lost and claims were made for eleven Japanese bombers and three fighters in the battle.

Realizing now that American planes were based in their back yard, the Japanese followed with a strafing raid on the following day. They were met not only by P-38s but also by the new P-47 Republic Thunderbolt, flown by the 348th Fighter Group led by Colonel Neel Kearby. The Japanese lost nine fighters (of the approximate fifteen dispatched) and five bombers (of sixteen). American losses

Japanese Mitsubishi, Type 97, "Sally," heavy bomber which occasionally operated as a fighter.

(U. S. AIR FORCE)

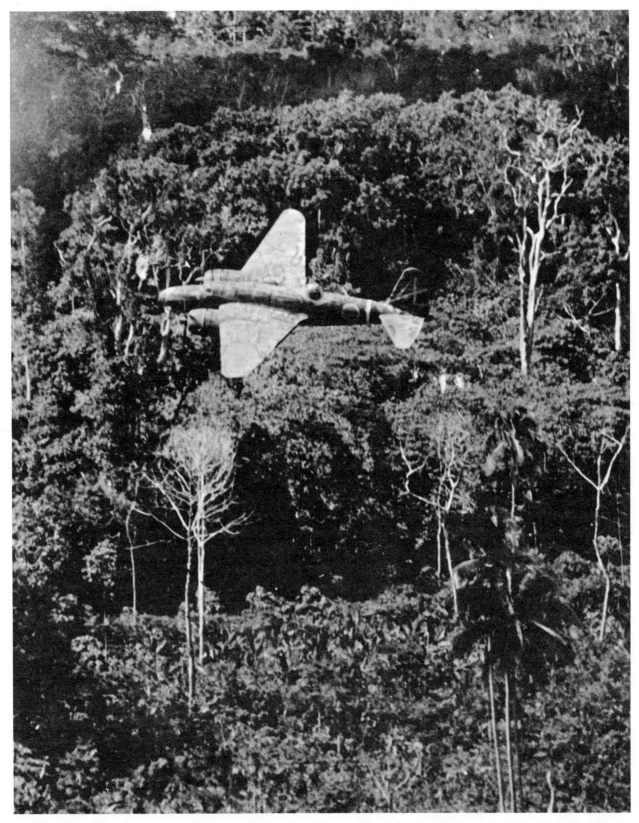

A Sally taking off during a Fifth Air Force attack on a Japanese base in New Guinea. Shortly after it was destroyed by another bomber, a B-25 Mitchell.

(U. S. AIR FORCE)

takeoff. No doubt the Japanese planned to avenge the midnight bombings by the B-17s and B-24s. Half a hundred fighters, the escort, also lined up on other runways getting ready to take off. The lead bomber had begun its run down the strip when Hall roared in with his potent Mitchells.

A shattering burst from his nose guns caught the Japanese bomber still on the runway. Enveloped in flame, it crashed to the ground and rendered the runway inoperable for any further takeoffs. The 8th and 13th Squadrons, seventeen planes altogether, led by Hall, in the words of Kenney, "swept over the field like a giant scythe," blasting at the lined-up bombers and fighters with their nose guns and drop-

ping parafrags in their wake. The bombs wafted down among the smoking, burning wreckage, further detonating aircraft and ripping up planes. Fuel drums burst into flame, adding their liquid propulsion to the holocaust. Those antiaircraft positions missed by the strafers were deracinated by the parafrags. In just minutes, the airdrome at Boram was left a burning, wreckage-strewn charnel house. Men of the 8th Squadron believed that they had left fifteen of the sixty or so planes they had counted on the strips totally destroyed and over twenty-five burning. The 13th Squadron was more expansive, claiming that of eighty or so aircraft it had counted all had been destroyed or severely damaged.

Parafrags falling on a Japanese airstrip at Boram, New Guinea. Earlier attacks have already decapitated palm trees and burned up bombers (lower left); at *upper right a fuel truck about to service a Zero will be the victim of the floating bombs.*

(U. S. AIR FORCE)

At the same time, twelve B-25s of the 90th Squadron (3rd Bombardment Group) were attending to Wewak proper. The surprise attack caught a number of Japanese fighters on the ground and left half of them, about fifteen, destroyed or damaged. Those Oscars (the Nakajima Ki.43) which got off the ground were driven off by the gunners in the Mitchells, leaving nothing to be done by the escorting P-38s, of which there were no less than eighty-five hovering around waiting for something to do.

Of the twenty-six B-25s which had taken off from Port Moresby that morning, assigned targets at Dagua and But, only three managed to rendezvous, because of bad weather. These three continued on to Dagua (But was not hit at all) and, despite their small number, created a burning shambles with guns and more than a hundred parafrags. Gunners shot down one intercepting Oscar, but at least seventeen lay in burning junk heaps on the ground when the Mitchells returned to Port Moresby.

Precise damage could not of course be estimated, but following what the Japanese came to call "The Black Day of August 17," there was little of the Japanese Air Force remaining in the Wewak area. But that did not mean it no longer existed, as was revealed on the following day, when similar strikes were made on Wewak. The weather spoiled the efforts of the heavy bombers to some extent; of the

Japanese antiaircraft gunners seek shelter from the bombing-strafing Fifth Air Force Mitchells as a parafrag drifts toward their gun position. (U. S. AIR FORCE)

A "sight to gladden the heart of a strafer": Mitchells seeding the airbase at Dagua, New Guinea; smoke from a burning "Helen" bomber fills the air as three neatly lined-up "Tony" fighters await their turn.
(U. S. AIR FORCE)

forty-nine which took off only twenty-six succeeded in bombing Wewak and Boram. The 3rd Bombardment Group followed with another low-level strafing and parafrag attack. The airdrome appearing to be pretty well taken care of, the 3rd swung out to sea, struck at some cargo vessels anchored off Wewak, and then blazed supply dumps at Boram.

The 38th Bombardment Group had been assigned Dagua. Major Ralph Cheli of the 405th Squadron led the attack, which was intercepted by about a dozen Japanese fighters, Zekes and Oscars, several miles out of Dagua. The fighters furiously attacked the low-flying Mitchells, concentrating on Major Cheli's flight. Within seconds, one of the B-25s was forced to pull away because of damage and fluttered back to base. An Oscar which had attacked this plane swung into Major Cheli's also and sent a burst along the right wing and engine. Flame erupted from the Mitchell as Cheli continued leading the

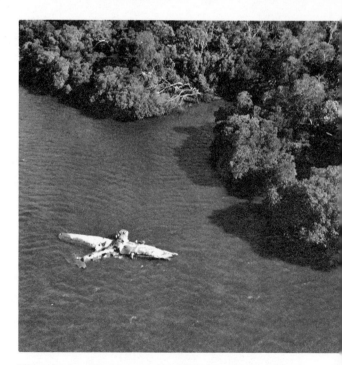

Though the tide was turning, the air war over Boram, Wewak, and Dagua was not one-sided. Here is a Mitchell down in the water off New Guinea.
(HENRY W. UHLIG/U. S. AIR FORCE)

B-25s toward Dagua, still two miles away. Rather than pull up, Cheli remained in place at the head of the squadron leading the attack. His leaving the formation at this critical point might easily have upset the strike; he chose to remain near the ground (too low to take to parachutes) with himself and his crew in the burning Mitchell.

The plane spouted flame as Cheli swept in over Dagua, strafing and dropping parafrags. This completed, Cheli instructed his wingman to take over the formation for the return flight, saying that he would attempt to bring the burning plane down into the sea. He turned and made for the water, reached it in fact, but it was too late. The flames had reached

a fuel tank and the explosion ripped a wing off the B-25, which crashed into the Pacific. Ralph Cheli was awarded the Medal of Honor for his action that day.

These two days of low-level attacks had succeeded in seriously crippling the Japanese aerial potential in New Guinea. By the end of the month it was estimated that more than two hundred aircraft had been destroyed on the ground alone (the revised, more precise figure was 175, which is still impres-

Troops of the 503rd Parachute Infantry float down upon Nadzab, New Guinea, in MacArthur's move to eliminate the Japanese stronghold at Lae.

(U. S. AIR FORCE)

The death of a Zero over Salamaua south of Nadzab and Lae about a week before the latter fell to MacArthur's forces. (U. S. AIR FORCE)

sive). Claims were made for 126 Japanese aircraft accounted for in combat against the loss of five Mitchells, four B-24s, and thirteen fighters in combat and by accident during the month of August.

Marilinan, from which attacks could be mounted, served also as an emergency field and refueling depot for the fighters. Kenney concluded the field "had already paid for itself."

By late August MacArthur was confident that his forces could strike at another Japanese stronghold up the spine of New Guinea—Lae in the Huon Gulf. Amphibious troops, both Australian and American, went ashore near the village of Hopoi to set up a beachhead about fourteen miles east of Lae on the morning of September 4, 1943. This was preceded by naval and air bombardment of the landing area as well as concentrated bombing of Japanese positions in New Guinea and Rabaul. Even so, some Japanese aerial activity interfered slightly with the Lae landing, although at heavy cost, for Kenney's P-38s and P-47s swarmed around for in-

terceptions. Within four hours of the opening of the operation some 7800 troops had been put ashore along with their weapons and supplies.

The next morning the C-47s of the 54th Troop Carrier Wing lifted off the strips at Port Moresby carrying Australian troops and the men of the U. S. 503rd Paratroop Regiment. The unarmed transports, seventy-nine C-47s carrying about seventeen hundred men, were met by their first escorts over Thirty-Mile airdrome. As the armada proceeded, the escort eventually rose to a hundred fighters. Over Marilinan, just southwest of Lae, the C-47s formed into drop formation and flew to Nadzab, which flanked Lae to the west. What followed was one of the finest, most precise airdrops of the war, as, according to Kenney, MacArthur in his command B-17 observed "the show . . . jumping up and down like a kid." The paratroopers landed without meeting any resistance, and their C-47s returned to Port Moresby without the loss of a single plane. The Americans soon joined with the Australians and the area belonged to the Allies. Almost immediately construction of an air base was begun at Nadzab; Lae itself fell on September 16, 1943, and Kenney became proprietor of yet another major base.

Another way station like that at Marilinan was an airdrome constructed on Kiriwina, one of the Trobriand Islands, which lay almost directly east of Dobodura, New Guinea, and about 325 miles from Rabaul to the north. From the strips on Kiriwina, built by Royal Australian Air Force engineers, it would be possible for the B-25s to "stage" (refuel, etc.) before heading for Rabaul with weighty bomb loads. Fighters, primarily P-38s, were able to escort the bombers to Rabaul and not concern their pilots too much with fuel problems, for even if the Mitchells returned to New Guinea, the fighters could always land at Kiriwina. The heavy bombers could use Dobodura as their staging area. By October Kenney was ready to launch an offensive upon Rabaul similar in intensity to those with which he had been afflicting the Japanese along the northern coast of New Guinea.

Reconnaissance photograph of Vunakanau, one of the major Japanese air bases at Rabaul, New Britain (an island group east of New Guinea). This strip had already been visited by the Fifth Air Force as evidenced by wreckage. (U. S. AIR FORCE)

Rabaul had long been a prime target area, what with its several airdromes (two of which, at Lakunai, had been built by the Australians before the war), its harbor facilities, and warehouses in the city itself. As an important Japanese base, feeding men and matériel into New Guinea and the Solomons, Rabaul was also heavily protected: the estimate by early October 1943 was about 145 fighters, 124 bombers, and over 350 antiaircraft guns. The Japanese Navy had also installed quite efficient early warning radar systems. From Rabaul, too, bombing missions to New Guinea and to the Solomons were dispatched. In co-operation with the forces of Halsey's South Pacific units, and to assist in taking some of the pressure off the Allied Bougainville offensive in the Solomons, Kenney was determined to "take out Rabaul."

II

He had begun this task shortly after his arrival in the Pacific with the August 7, 1942, strike, which had consisted of thirteen 19th Bombardment Group Flying Fortresses. Rabaul had been under intermittent attack and regular reconnaissance since the previous January, in fact. From time to time Kenney would send a force of bombers to hit the shipping or airfields in the area; but it was a costly target. During the Buna campaign Kenney and his Bomber Command chief, Brigadier General Walker, agreed that striking at Rabaul's shipping would confute Japanese plans to send reinforcements to New Guinea. On one of these strikes, that of January 5, 1943, Walker disobeyed Kenney's orders and flew in one of the dozen bombers sent to bomb Rabaul Harbor. Although Kenney had ordered a dawn attack, Walker believed a noon attack would achieve higher accuracy. While this may have been true—for claims for no less than ten ships sunk or burning were made—the antiaircraft fire was murderous and attacks by defending Japanese fighters profuse, if not expert. However, two American bombers were lost, one of them carrying Walker. Apparently hit by flak, the B-17, with engine burning, lost altitude and attracted two Zeros, which followed the plane away from the main battle. That was the last seen of Walker's B-17 by those ten crews which returned to Port Moresby.

When it came time to intensify the Fifth Air Force's attention on Rabaul, a campaign scheduled to open the middle of October 1943, Kenney was able finally to plan a sizable attack. There were no dozen or so patched up B-17s now, but several squadrons each of Mitchells, P-38s, and B-24s—nearly 350 aircraft. This too was a tribute to the resourcefulness of Kenney, who, by whatever means, had built up his air force. He fought with MacArthur's staff, he fought with Arnold's staff in far-off Washington, he demanded, "squawked," to use his term, and simply took what he could. This affected supplies, matériel of all types from planes to food for his "kids." If Service of Supply, bogged down with red tape, would not issue fresh food to his front-line fliers, Kenney arranged for a fleet of aircraft to smuggle it in from Australia. While this infringed on rules and regulations, it made a great deal of difference to the men who fought in terms of health and morale. Kenney even blinked when refrigerators were flown into New Guinea labeled as aircraft engines; if anything, he no doubt initiated the shipment of contraband.

He regularly had to defend his men. When Service of Supply officers in Sydney complained of the behavior of Kenney's airmen on leave, indicating that it was time "these brats grew up and behaved themselves," Kenney lashed out at the complainants, in-

dicating that he didn't want his kids to get "old, fat, bald-headed and respectable like some people present because I was quite sure that, if they did they would no longer shoot down Nip planes and sink Nip boats."

In so many words, Kenney told the by now red-faced rear echeloners that since leave was granted to men who had been fighting the war, it was just too bad that their cavortings disturbed the slumber of the SOS. So far as he was concerned they could . . .

Just then MacArthur appeared in the doorway. Kenney stopped talking to say, "Good morning, General."

MacArthur studied the group for just a moment, then said, "Leave Kenney's Kids alone. I don't want to see them grow up either." Chuckling, but with great dignity, he left.

MacArthur enjoyed Kenney's at times gauche style, his bluntness, his unconventional handling of supply and command problems. It was as if the austere, limelighted MacArthur could unbend through Kenney. Soon he came to call Kenney "Buccaneer," in recognition of the airman's freewheeling, productive manner of operating. On the other hand, Kenney was popular also with his men, who admired his informal swashbuckling manner—and the fact that he never failed to go out on a limb for them, if necessary.

They, in turn, willingly went out on a limb for Kenney. Taking out Rabaul was one of those limbs. On the eve of the opening of the intensive campaign, Kenney wrote to Arnold, "This is the beginning of what I believe is the most decisive action initiated so far in this theater. We are out not only to gain control of the air over New Britain and New Ireland but to make Rabaul untenable for Jap shipping and to set up an air blockade of all the Jap forces in that area."

Because of the oncoming monsoon predicted by his weathermen, Kenney unleashed his bombers on October 12, 1943, three days ahead of the agreed-upon date of the official top-level meetings. The early morning phase of the attack was led by Lieutenant Colonel Clinton U. True, commanding officer of the 345th Bombardment Group, at the vanguard of more than a hundred strafer Mitchells. Flying low over the water to elude radar, the Mitchells crossed the Solomon Sea to Kiriwina (where the

The Fifth Air Force delivers parafrags to Vunakanau bomber revetments in Kenney's offensive on Rabaul.
(U. S. AIR FORCE)

P-38 escort was picked up) and swung around to approach Rabaul. As they came in at treetop level, the formations split: the forty Mitchells of the 3rd Group veered sharply to port, streaking for the airdrome at Rapopo, and the sixty-seven aircraft of the 38th and 345th Groups turned slightly, to pounce upon Vunakanau. The attacks followed the pattern of those at Wewak and Lae. The 3rd Group, for example, swept in in a succession of shallow Vs, about a dozen Mitchells across, with the Vs about a mile apart. Spraying the target area with their eight nose guns, the Mitchells roared over the airfields dropping their parafrags into revetments (con-

structed to protect aircraft from horizontal bomb blasts) and over the general dispersal area.

Surprise having apparently been achieved, the Mitchells encountered remarkably little opposition. Antiaircraft fire was neither persistent nor accurate. Fighters, however, attempted interception and in a battle over Vunakanau with Zekes (the more modern Zero) the Mitchell piloted by Lieutenant Sidney W. Crews, with engine aflame, crashed into the waters of St. George Channel. It was the only Mitchell lost in the attack.

As soon as the Mitchells had cleared the area, a dozen Australian Beaufighters of No. 30 Squadron swooped down to work over Rapopo and Tobera. One of these aircraft was knocked down by ground fire.

A Japanese bomber burns after a parafrag has alighted near it. (U. S. AIR FORCE)

Shortly after noon the B-24s of the 90th Bombardment Group came in high over Simpson Harbour to drop thousand-pound bombs on the shipping in the harbor. Zekes quickly rose to challenge the Liberators, and in the ensuing battle, which lasted for more than a half hour, two B-24s were lost, with gunners in the bombers claiming ten of the forty Zekes and Zeros attacking. The Liberators of the 43rd Group followed the 90th Group's planes (which drew off most of the Japanese fighters) and strung their bombs across the harbor. Crewmen reported burning ships and much confusion in Simpson Harbour and heavy but inaccurate antiaircraft fire. Escorting P-38s claimed twenty-six Japanese fighters shot down; the strafer-bombers estimated that no less than a hundred Japanese planes had been destroyed on the ground with another fifty badly damaged. The heavies claimed over a hundred ships of various sizes, function, and tonnages sunk or destroyed—rather optimistic claims, as revealed in later photoreconnaissance. Exact damages could not be known, in fact, because of the speed of the action and the smoke left in the target areas by the Mitchells. But the claims were not as critical as the fact that the big campaign on Rabaul had begun with a decided success and with a reasonably small loss.

Despite intermittent bad weather, which either canceled out strikes or interfered with missions, the Fifth Air Force continued pounding away at Rabaul. Unless Kenney maintained a constant assault the Japanese were able to repair damage and replace lost aircraft. Meanwhile, too, Japanese strikes were mounted upon Allied positions in New Guinea, to upset any plans for what appeared to the Japanese to be a softening-up prelude for an invasion of Rabaul. This clearly near-suicidal effort was never attempted, however. It was the fate of Rabaul to be bypassed, isolated, as were so many other Japanese strong points on the way to Tokyo.

The ships in Simpson Harbour were as important as targets as were the aircraft on the five major airdromes of Rabaul. When the weather grounded planes, the ships continued to bring in supplies and troops. It devolved upon the 8th Photo Squadron, flying converted P-38s (the F-5), to keep an eye on the weather as well as the installations at Rabaul. Reconnaissance had revealed a concentration of ships in Simpson Harbour toward the end of October, making an attack from low level (always more effective than high-altitude bombing against ships) next on the Fifth Air Force agenda.

The weather caused the scrubbing of several missions to Simpson Harbour at the end of October. November came and the bad weather seemed fated to continue; the missions of the first and second were also canceled. But then, P-38s in the Rabaul area reported, after the morning mission of November 2, 1943, had been scrubbed, that not only was the weather over Rabaul promising, but that Simpson Harbour was filled with ships: a destroyer, a tender, and about twenty assorted transports. The mission was on again.

Because of the sudden shift in plans, not many Fifth Air Force aircraft were dispatched from New Guinea and the base at Kiriwina. According to Kenney there were seventy-five (Air Force historians say eighty) B-25 strafers and fifty-seven P-38s (historians claim eighty). The actual numbers assume a certain importance because of the intensity

The attack on Rabaul's Simpson Harbour, November 2, 1943. As shore installations burn in the background, *a skip-bombing Mitchell sweeps across the harbor as ship burns.* (U. S. AIR FORCE)

Rabaul goes up in smoke after the November 2 mission to Simpson Harbour. (U. S. AIR FORCE)

of the battle which ensued. It is likely that Kenney's are closest to the actual figures because the squadrons participating were not up to full strength.

Nine B-25 squadrons took part in the attack: the 8th, 13th, and 90th (of the 3rd Bombardment Group); the 71st and 405th (38th Bombardment Group); and the 498th, 499th, 500th, and 501st of the 345th Bombardment Group. Furnishing fighter cover for the strafers were six fighter squadrons: the 9th (49th Fighter Group); the 39th (35th Fighter Group); the 80th (8th Fighter Group); and the 431st, 432nd, and 433rd of the 475th Fighter Group.

By 11 A.M. the force was air-borne and headed for Rabaul. The P-38s of the 39th and 80th Squadrons opened the attack by swooping in upon the harbor to shoot up the antiaircraft installations there. Major Benjamin Fridge followed with the four B-25 squadrons of the 345th Group to strafe the gun emplacements around the harbor, drop Kenney Cocktails (the phosphorus bombs), and sweep over to

Lakunai airdrome and do the same there. The Kenney Cocktails laid a screen of smoke over the land-based guns and ignited Rabaul itself.

But unlike the earlier squadrons, the planes of the 345th ran into tough interception and intense anti-aircraft fire. Several Mitchells were shot up during the attack and three were lost. The initial attack, however, prepared the way for the remaining five squadrons of B-25s, led by Major John P. Henebry, which had time to circle over Rabaul (impossible normally because of the harbor guns) for an effective run on the shipping in the harbor.

As Henebry dropped down upon Simpson Harbour, two Japanese destroyers which lay in the mouth of a river opened up on the forty-one Mitchells. This plus the smoke of the already burning ships disturbed, to some degree, the plan of attack. Despite this the strafers, breaking up into small units, poured fire in upon the ships in the harbor. Some of the Japanese ships shot directly into the water in the path of the approaching American planes, geysering water into the very cockpits of the B-25s. At the same time, especially aggressive Zeros pounced upon Henebry's squadrons. These fighters proved more effective than any encountered by the Fifth Air Force in quite some time. They were veteran Japanese Imperial Navy pilots of the 1st Koku Sentai (Carrier Division) from old Admiral Nagumo's carriers *Shokaku, Zuikaku,* and *Zuiho.* It had been a long time since the Fifth Air Force men had seen so many Zeros in the air at one time.

Kenney, who called this battle "the toughest, hardest-fought engagement of the war" for his air force, estimated that the Japanese put up "between 125 and 150 fighters" that day. Their numbers, and skill as pilots, enabled the Japanese to break through the P-38 escort to get at the Mitchells bombing the harbor. Despite the persistent Zeros and the ground fire, the Mitchells slashed at the ships, striking more than forty, of which twenty-four were hit by bombs and seventeen strafed.

In the melee, six B-25s and one P-38 were knocked down into Simpson Harbour. Henebry's plane was so badly shot up that when he left the battle area, his B-25 was full of holes and one engine was gone. With extraordinary airmanship, Henebry skimmed and yawed away from Rabaul until the Mitchell fell into the Pacific just short of Kiriwina. Henebry and his crew were rescued shortly after.

One of Henebry's squadron commanders, Major Raymond H. Wilkins, did not get away from Rabaul. Leading the 8th Squadron, the last to attack, Wilkins flew on the formation's left flank, which brought him under fire from cruisers near the shore. The area by this time, actually only twelve minutes after the initial attack, was a turmoil of smoke, machine-gun tracers, water spray, and concentrated antiaircraft fire.

"Smoke from bombs dropped by preceding aircraft necessitated a last-second revision of tactics on his part," Wilkins' Medal of Honor citation reads, "which still enabled his squadron to strike at vital shipping targets but forced it to approach through concentrated fire, and increased the danger of Major Wilkins' left-flank position.

"His airplane was hit almost immediately, the right wing damaged, and control rendered extremely difficult. Although he could have withdrawn he held fast and led his squadron in to the attack."

Wilkins' forward-firing eight-gun battery roared to life as he "strafed a group of small harbor vessels, and then, at low-level, attacked an enemy destroyer. His thousand-pound bomb struck squarely amidships, causing the vessel to explode. Although antiaircraft fire from this vessel had seriously damaged his left vertical stabilizer, he refused to deviate from his course. From below mast-head height he attacked a transport of some nine thousand tons, scoring a hit which engulfed the ship in flames. Bombs expended he began to withdraw his squadron.

"A heavy cruiser barred the path. Unhesitatingly, to neutralize the cruiser's guns and attract their fire, he went in for a strafing run. His damaged stabilizer was completely shot off." With his directional control all but gone, Wilkins might easily have flown into the path of the Mitchells flying alongside him. He rolled the plane slightly, with what little aileron control he still had, to avoid colliding with his wing mates. In doing this he exposed the belly and full wing surfaces to the heavy fire erupting from "those damned cruisers." In an instant the Mitchell's left wing crumpled and the bomber smashed into the sea.

Wilkins and his crew were among the forty-five men lost in the attack: one of the heaviest tolls suffered by the Fifth Air Force. Eight bombers and nine fighters were lost (although four of the pilots of the latter were found and crews of three bombers, such as that of Henebry, were picked up). A Mitchell and three P-38s, badly damaged in the fighting, cracked up while landing at Dobodura. It had been an expensive "show."

Simpson Harbour had been left a smoking shambles when the last Mitchell of the 8th Squadron passed through its hail of fire. But any accurate assessment of the damage would have been questionable. The first official communiqué claimed fifteen Japanese vessels, of various types, sunk and an additional thirteen damaged (after the war the Japanese admitted to three merchant vessels, a minesweeper, and two small ships sunk and damage to a ten-thousand-ton tanker). Whatever the differences, the attack proved costly to the Japanese also.

Besides the damage to shipping in the harbor (and tankers were an especially precious commodity at the time), the town of Rabaul was also set aflame, which accounted for the destruction of supplies. In

As the fighting progressed all around Rabaul and Simpson Harbour, Kenney Cocktails fanned over Lakunai *gun positions (center and right bottom), scourging the hapless gun crews.* (U. S. AIR FORCE)

the air fighting, bombers and fighters claimed sixty-eight Japanese planes shot down; the strafers claimed an additional sixteen destroyed on the ground at Lakunai plus ten float planes which were left burning in the harbor. So, if the battle had been hard on the Fifth Air Force, it was also a definite blow to the Japanese.

By the end of November, with Halsey's carriers closing in on Rabaul, Kenney relinquished the further "neutralization of Rabaul" to the South Pacific forces, which included the recently formed Thirteenth Air Force besides the Marine and Navy pilots. Although Rabaul was never invaded, any such attempt would have been costly in the extreme, it was not completely taken out either. But the incessant attacks upon it eventually forced the withdrawal of air units stationed there by February 20, 1944. Left behind were nearly 100,000 ground troops, who waited in 350 miles of tunnels and caves. It was one of the good fortunes of war that the Joint Chiefs did not order an invasion of Rabaul. Had they, "Tarawa, Iwo Jima and Okinawa would have faded to pale pink in comparison with the blood that would have flowed" in an attempted assault on Rabaul, in the opinion of Samuel Eliot Morison. Even so, the blood continued to flow until the end.

Meanwhile, Kenney gave his attention to MacAr-

A low-flying Mitchell, of the 345th Bomb Group, Thirteenth Air Force, catches a Japanese "frigate" (destroyer escort) off the coast of China. In moments the B-25s of the group, known as the "Air Apaches," finish off the ship which capsizes. (U. S. AIR FORCE)

thur's advance up the coast of New Guinea, employing the methods used upon Rabaul as he went.

III

The attacks by strafers, the deliverers of Kenney Cocktails, parafrags, and the heavy bombs, were protected whenever possible by fighters. Kenney's fighter pilots were among the most colorful of the war, and the so-called "Ace of Aces" of all American wars was one of Kenney's Kids. Richard Ira Bong, "a blond, blue-eyed cherub" from Madison, Wisconsin, first came to Kenney's attention in San Francisco. Kenney was then commanding the Fourth Air Force when word came to his office that one of his pilots "had been looping the loop around the center span of the Golden Gate Bridge in a P-38 fighter plane and waving to the stenographic help in the office buildings as he flew along Market Street."

From nearby Oakland a lady complained of having her washing blown off the line by a low-flying aircraft. Though angry and a bit embarrassed over the performance of one of his pilots, Kenney was also delighted. Kenney himself had nearly been dismissed from the Air Service in the summer of 1917 for flying under the bridges of New York's East River.

Kenney laced into the youthful pilot, a "boy about five feet six, with a round, pink baby face and the bluest, most innocent eyes," affecting his harshest voice and sternest expression. He reminded Bong of the trouble he had caused, which would make it necessary for Kenney to talk with everyone, from the governor on down to the lady with the washing.

Then Kenney's curiosity got the better of him. "By the way," he said to Bong, "wasn't the air pretty rough down in the street around the second-story level?"

The innocence vanished from Bong's eyes. "Yes, sir, it was kind of rough, but it was easy to control the plane." He then launched into a speech on the excellent aileron control of the P-38 before realizing that he was in his commanding general's office for an entirely different reason.

Kenney rather dramatically began tearing up the pile of complaints that had accumulated on his desk thanks to this cherubic "airplane jockey." Threatening the by now incredulous Bong with in-

Richard Bong, P-38 fighter pilot, New Guinea, 1943. Bong would become the American "ace of aces" with a total of forty confirmed air-to-air victories.

(U. S. AIR FORCE)

stant dismissal from the Air Force should he ever repeat his performance, Kenney added further reprimand: Bong was ordered to report to the lady near Oakland.

And "if that woman has any washing to be hung out on the line, you do it for her. Then you hang around being useful—mowing a lawn or something—and when the clothes are dry, take them off the line and bring them into the house. And don't drop any of them on the ground or you will have to wash them over again."

Almost immediately after the incident, Kenney was on his way to the Pacific and when he placed a request with Arnold for fifty P-38 pilots, he specifically requested that Bong be among them.

In Kenney's professional eye, Bong (who was then twenty-two) combined those several qualities which add up to a superb fighter pilot. Quick reflexes, good physical condition, a sense of joy in the very idea of flight, an understanding of aircraft and its limitations, as well as his own. Aggressiveness too was an important psychophysiological component. Along with this must be a self-confidence bordering on an overwhelming sense of invincibility. The hesitant, too cerebral fighter pilot did not generally survive. Swooping down for a screaming attack, most often as not upon an unaware enemy—for in reality, for all of the scorekeeping, combat aviation was no clean sport—the fighter was too preoccupied with air speed, angle of attack, getting a bead on the enemy aircraft to consider the outcome of this attack as less than fatal for the enemy.

Like so many other American fighter pilots, Bong was not, in the beginning at least, a very good shot. He actually completed his first tour of missions, with more than twenty "kills" to his credit, before he attended a school for training in aerial gunnery. The bulk of Bong's forty official victories can be attributed to his courage (another term for aggressiveness or self-confidence), his skill with the P-38, and a willingness to work as part of a team.

Early in the Pacific war it became obvious that the dogfighting tactics of the First World War were suicidal with the Zero, which could dance circles around the heavier American fighters. "Defense against Jap fighters is resolved around the superior speed of our fighters," Bong pointed out, and it was that difference between the machines, his and the Japanese, that he exploited, not individual flying abilities. The Japanese were better pilots—and had much sharper vision than early Allied propaganda intimated. So were their aircraft better under certain conditions; because they were less ruggedly constructed, weight and speed were important in battle. As Bong observed, "An indicated airspeed never less than 250 miles per hour in combat is good life insurance."

Even so, there were sudden unknowns confronting even an experienced pilot—and it was these too which often saved him. One of these incidents occurred to Bong even after he had already achieved acedom. He and his wingman intercepted a Japanese bomber formation, escorted by Zeros, over the Buna area of New Guinea. The bombers seemed beautifully set up for a quick, slashing attack. "Any number of Nips," he once wrote, "can be safely attacked from above. Dive on the group, pick a definite plane as your target, and concentrate on him. . . ."

As he concentrated on his bomber, Bong, with the fighter pilot's instinct for searching the air around him, came to a sudden shocking realization. On his wing was not a twin-boomed P-38, but a Zero with a large red circle on its side. In seconds it could slip behind him and begin firing with its cannon.

Chopping the throttle of one of his engines, Bong suddenly flipped away in a careening dive. Checking his rear-view mirror, and not seeing a Zero, he leveled out at five thousand feet. Suddenly, there it was again, pulling up behind him, but too distant for accurate shooting. Bong flipped the P-38 once again and dived for the water. The Zero could not follow him there—it might plunge into the Pacific if it did, or else pull apart in the high-speed dive.

Japanese bombers ("Sally") in the gun camera of an American pilot. While thus occupied once Richard Bong acquired himself a Zero for a wingman.

(U. S. AIR FORCE)

Bong opened the throttles and raced over the water, glancing again into the mirror. He had left the Zero way behind; maybe now he could deal with the persistent Japanese. He snapped the plane into a tight turn and found himself in the middle of a nine-plane Japanese formation he had not seen until that instant.

There was nothing in the books to cover this situation. Bong relied on instinct as he yanked the great plane's nose into the path of the lead Japanese aircraft. A short burst from Bong's gun blew the Zero out of his way. This apparently had shaken the remaining eight Zeros, for their fire was not accurate. Bong ripped the P-38 through the scattering Japanese formation and shot and detonated another Zero. Ramming his engines at full throttle, he climbed for altitude, loosing another burst at a passing Zero. The Japanese plane paused, emitted smoke, and fluttered away from the battle.

By this time Bong was far from the dispersed Japanese planes and heading for home base.

Despite the preoccupation with keeping score of kills, the true function of the fighters was, of course, protecting the bombers during the attacks upon shipping or such bases as Rabaul, Lae, Wewak, and the other steps toward the Philippines. Lone-eagle fighting generally ended in the death of the eagle.

The system of fighting in pairs may have denied a wingman his share of "credits" (and there were those pilots who resented it), but it did preserve life. But not forever.

Once the American pilots began adding up kills it was inevitable that a certain rivalry would grow among the pilots. It was a good-natured, locker-room kind of competitiveness, this obsession with kills, except that instead of touchdowns men's lives were at stake.

When Bong passed the score of First World War ace Captain Eddie Rickenbacker, the latter sent the young ace a case of scotch with which to celebrate. This resulted in quite a tempest in a scotch glass, for a flood of complaints and criticism deluged Kenney for permitting this (in fact, Bong himself did not drink and was more delighted with a gift of Coca-Cola from Generals Arnold and MacArthur). The back-home do-gooders could not reconcile themselves to the fact of the "boys'" drinking, although they readily accepted the fact that they were out killing their fellow man. Wartime provides the setting for any number of moral incongruities, with the most pietistic leading the pack.

When Bong arrived in New Guinea to embark upon his legendary career as a fighter pilot, the top-scoring ace of the time was Boyd David Wagner, who was best known as "Buzz," with a score of eight. A veteran of the early Pacific fighting, Wagner returned to the United States only to die in an accidental crash during a takeoff at Eglin Air Force Base.

Bong's rival during his initial tour was another youngster, Captain Thomas J. Lynch of Catasauqua, Pennsylvania. Lynch had led the first P-38 mission (December 27, 1942), twelve in all, from the Laloki airstrip near Port Moresby. Intercepting a Japanese bomber and fighter formation over Dobodura, the P-38 pilots returned from the battle claiming no less than fifteen Japanese planes. Bong, Lynch, and another future ace, Lieutenant Kenneth C. Sparks, claimed two apiece. Although the green fighters committed any number of tactical errors— firing from too great a distance, attempting to dogfight with a Zero—their initiation into battle had been exciting and without loss. Kenney, in reporting the battle debut of the P-38 to Arnold, noted that "morale in that squadron [the 9th of the 49th Fighter Group] is so high it almost scares you."

Another group, the 348th, had arrived in New Guinea around the end of June 1943. The commander, Colonel Neel E. Kearby, looked to Kenney "like money in the bank." The 348th was equipped with the Republic P-47 ("Thunderbolt," or "Jug") and Kearby was anxious to prove what the as yet unpopular aircraft could do. The P-47 was a hulk of an aircraft, the largest single-engine one-man fighter of the war. It did not have the range of the P-38 (until fitted with belly tanks), was difficult to maneuver, had a weak landing gear, and could, in a power dive, freeze the controls so that the pilot could not pull out. Or if he did, the action could tear the tail section away. Despite these drawbacks, the P-47 properly manned became one of the outstanding fighters of the war.

Kearby, one of its earliest exponents, was anxious to show what the plane, his group, and he himself could do. He had barely met Kenney before he asked about "scores," the implication being, Kenney believed, that he "wanted to know who he had to beat." It was not until August that the 348th

Neel E. Kearby, who commanded the 348th Fighter Group, and who proved that the P-47 "Thunderbolt" was a formidable aircraft in the Pacific.

(U. S. AIR FORCE)

Fighter Group's Thunderbolts were ready for action. Then in September, during the air fighting over Lea and the subsequent (September 5, 1943) taking of Nadzab by American paratroopers, Kearby got his chance. With a wingman as company Kearby dived on two Japanese planes, a bomber and a fighter. With his wingman following, Kearby dropped the Thunderbolt upon the enemy planes about four thousand feet below. The two planes were flying along rather close together, the bomber in the lead with the Zero following. Kearby squinted in the sight and shot off a long, exploratory burst as his wingman held his fire and twisted his neck looking for other Japanese fighters.

To the surprise of both wingman and Kearby a wing ripped off the fighter and the bomber ex-

ploded before their eyes. By the end of September Kearby's score had grown to eight, one half of Bong's score at the time.

Multiple victories seemed to be a Kearby specialty, for on October 11 he gave an amazing demonstration which won him the Medal of Honor. During a fighter sweep over the Wewak area in company with three others, Major Raymond K. Gallagher, Captain John T. Moore, and Captain William D. Dunham, Kearby sighted a single Japanese plane below them.

Kearby led his flight down upon the lone Zero and in seconds sent it down burning (the eight .50-caliber guns of the P-47 literally tore the flimsy plane apart). Then as the four Thunderbolts pulled up out of their dive they saw ahead of them a large formation of Japanese fighters and bombers, about forty-five planes in all.

Kearby plunged into the formation in an instant, the three others following. The heavy P-47 lumbered through the astonished Japanese spouting fire: three enemy planes burst into flame within minutes. Then, kicking rudder, Kearby turned to see that two Zeros had got onto the tail of one of his flight. He roared in and with two bursts sent the two Japanese down burning. Instinctively he scanned the air around him and saw that a Zero had begun a dive upon another P-47. Kearby whipped the guns into the enemy plane, which collapsed, falling like a bird with a broken spine.

Realizing that they were getting low on fuel, Kearby called his men in—all were safe. Besides Kearby's seven victories, two more had been accounted for by other members of the flight and another had been seen leaving the battle on fire. Because it had not been seen to crash this was claimed as a "probable." Discounting this one, it meant that the Japanese had lost nine planes to the four Thunderbolts in a single action.

But there was an additional hitch. Kearby's gun camera had run out of film in mid-attack on the seventh plane and there was no "official" evidence, the three other pilots then being occupied themselves, that the seventh plane had been destroyed. So Kearby was credited with an official six victories in a single battle (the record to that date was the Navy's Lieutenant Edward "Butch" O'Hare, who had shot down five Japanese bombers in a single action). For his feat, Kearby received the Medal of

Honor and his score stood at fourteen, only three less than Bong's.

Shortly after, Bong was sent home for a rest (with a score then of twenty-one), and while he was away Kearby's total rose to twenty. At this time Bong's other rival, Thomas Lynch, had a score of sixteen (he too had been sent back home for a rest), so that the rivalry of these three aces now became intense.

When all three were in operation their individual scores were watched daily; by the beginning of March 1944 Bong and Kearby were tied (with twenty-two) and Lynch trailed with nineteen.

Whether or not the desire to be top ace blunted Kearby's customary vigilance, or whether it was a simple matter of running out of luck, would be difficult to ascertain. On March 4, 1944, Kearby was again leading a four-plane flight (Major Samuel Blair, Captain William Dunham, and Captain William Banks), this time over Wewak, New Guinea. Sighting a fifteen-plane Japanese formation, Kearby ordered an attack, the first assault of which sent one enemy plane down under his guns. He had broken the tie.

Thomas J. Lynch, one of Richard Bong's friendly rivals and battle companions. (U. S. AIR FORCE)

Turning, he rammed back into the battle and with a long shot, knocked another Zero down. Kearby was now official Ace of Aces. Then three Zeros converged upon his Thunderbolt. Dunham and Banks swept in with guns firing, each taking one of the Zeros off Kearby's tail. But the third from close up fired a burst of cannon directly into the cockpit of the P-47. It tipped on its nose and fell directly into the jungle; no parachute was seen. Obviously Neel Kearby was dead in the plane.

Ironically, on that same day Bong had destroyed two enemy aircraft; the score was still tied. Lynch with nineteen victories was now Bong's closest rival.

At this stage, Lynch—a lieutenant colonel—and Bong—a captain—had teamed up. They had been taken out of their regular squadrons and placed upon the staff of General Paul Wurtsmith, commander of Kenney's Fighter Command. Lynch was nominally Wurtsmith's operations officer and Bong his assistant. Thus it was hoped to keep the two fighters out of combat as much as possible and preserve their experience, which could be transferred to the new pilots coming into the Pacific.

This worked on paper, but it was difficult to keep the two men out of battle. They either went off together, or attached themselves to other squadrons and continued to add to their scores. They remained, as they did at the time of Kearby's death, Bong: twenty-four, Lynch: nineteen.

Just five days after Kearby's last fight, Bong and Lynch took off on one of their two-man hunts. Over Tadji, New Guinea, they surprised another two-man combat team and each took out one. There being no other Japanese aircraft in the sky, they pointed their P-38s down toward the water, where they spotted a Japanese ship, a corvette obviously headed for Hollandia. It was the best they could find, so they swept down upon the vessel. Raking the deck with .50-caliber bullets, the P-38s dived and pulled away, dived and pulled away as the guns on the ship's deck traded fire with them.

Suddenly Bong noticed that Lynch had turned away and headed for shore; an engine trailed smoke. Even more suddenly one of the propellers tore away, and as Bong watched in horror, he saw Lynch struggling out of the cockpit, ready to jump. Before he and his chute were free of the plane, the P-38 detonated. If Lynch had had a chance, the

Despite the superiority of American air power over New Guinea, attacking Japanese strongholds was not without hazard. In this series of photographs a Fifth

Air Force Havoc attacking Kokas, New Guinea, is hit by antiaircraft fire and plunges into the water.

(U. S. AIR FORCE)

flame of the explosion canceled that—the chute certainly burned and Lynch, if not already dead, fell to his death. Bong circled the area for signs of life (something he realized was futile), but there were no indications that Lynch had survived. He returned to his base and Kenney, concerned with Bong's morale, sent him to Australia, ostensibly to ferry a newly arrived P-38 back to New Guinea. But Kenney saw to it that the depot commander would not have one ready for two weeks.

By early April Bong had returned, and by the twelfth, upon adding two more kills to his credit in a battle over Hollandia, he had passed the score of Rickenbacker, making him the American Ace of Aces of both world wars. Kenney quickly took him out of combat, partly because there was some concern from Washington over the recent deaths of Kearby and Lynch and the loss of their "invaluable

services." Bong was returned to the United States at this point to be reunited with his family, his fiancée, Army public relations officers—and to study gunnery. He was to return to the Pacific as an instructor upon completion of this course.

Meanwhile, a new rival had arisen: Major Thomas Buchanan McGuire, Jr. When he arrived in the Pacific, in the spring of 1943, McGuire was assigned to Bong's own unit, the 49th Fighter Group. Bong's score was then eight. In time McGuire was reassigned to the 475th Fighter Group to serve in the 431st Squadron. A fine pilot, McGuire quickly revealed himself as one of the outstanding air fighters in the Pacific.

But it seemed to be his fate that he always remained eight victories behind Bong. Even when Bong was away from combat, McGuire himself was also out of things with various jungle illnesses. "I'll

Thomas B. McGuire, Jr. (here an air cadet), one of Kenney's most aggressive "kids," who risked his life— and lost it—trying to aid a fellow pilot.

(U. S. AIR FORCE)

bet," he once told Kenney, "when this war is over, they'll call me Eight Behind McGuire."

In time McGuire became commander of the 431st Squadron and his victory score mounted rapidly. "A fighter pilot must be aggressive," he believed. "The enemy on the defensive gives you the advantage, as he is trying to evade you, and not shoot you down. Never break your formation into less than two-ship elements. A man by himself is a liability. . . . On the defensive, keep up your speed.

"Go in close, and then when you think you are too close, go in closer."

McGuire was an excellent teacher and conscientious in looking after green pilots. All through Bong's combat career, McGuire trailed his victory tally, but it was obvious that he might eventually overtake the top ace, for the word went out that Bong must be taken out of combat. Following Bong's return from the United States he was supposed to instruct, not fight—except in self-defense. By late December 1944, when MacArthur had indeed returned to the Philippines, Bong's score had grown into the thirties. If the Japanese air forces had

petered out over New Guinea, there was still fight left in them over the Philippines. Bong therefore had to "defend" himself rather frequently, even if he only went along to observe how a squadron he had trained in gunnery performed on a routine patrol.

Within hours of arriving at Tacloban, Bong was "forced to defend himself," in the words of Kenney's report to Arnold, and shot down his thirty-first Japanese plane. The following day, while on a reconnaissance mission to find possible sites for airfields in the Tacloban vicinity, he accounted for two more Japanese aircraft within view of the Allied airdrome.

Arnold wired Kenney: "Major Bong's excuses in matter of shooting down three more Nips noted with happy skepticism by this headquarters. Subject officer incorrigible. In Judge Advocate's opinion, he is liable under Articles of War 122." This referred to willful or negligent damage to enemy equipment or personnel.

Tacloban was a busy place indeed, for when McGuire arrived there in early October (1943), it was just in time for a tangle with a Japanese fighter formation. The twenty P-38s, warned by radio of the approaching ten Japanese fighters, shot down six and drove the rest off. One of the victims was McGuire's twenty-third victory. Elated upon landing, McGuire said, "This is the kind of place I like, where you have to shoot 'em down so you can land on your own airdrome! Say, how many has Bong got now?"

The slender, little major learned he was now ten behind. With Bong himself in the area, McGuire jokingly kept an eye on him, muttering words about taking off "to protect his interests." The two men were good friends and teamed up to go "Nip hunting." Now and then McGuire "permitted" Bong to accompany his squadron on regular patrols during which each shared in the kills.

When Bong's official score reached forty (his actual score was probably much higher), Kenney decided to take him out of combat. He had flown 146 combat missions and had nearly 400 hours of combat time. He had lived a charmed life and Kenney felt it was time to stop tempting fate. Bong was reluctant, hoping to bring his score to an even fifty, but Kenney was unyielding.

Bong would be sent home to rest, to marry the girl back home, and to get into an entirely new concept in aviation, the jet plane. In order not to spoil his stateside reception, Kenney grounded McGuire, who had finally broken his "eight behind" jinx.

"You look tired to me," Kenney told McGuire.

"General, I never felt better in my life. I've gained five pounds in the last month. Besides, I'm only two behind—"

"That's just it," Kenney told McGuire. "You are tired and you won't be rested enough to fly again until I hear that Bong is back in the United States and has been greeted as the top-scoring ace of the war." Kenney explained that he did not want Bong to arrive in San Francisco to be greeted with "Hello, Number Two, how's the war going?"

McGuire laughed and understood Kenney's point, saying he certainly did not want to spoil anything for Bong. He promised to take a few days off to rest, although he seemed quite anxious for Bong to be on his way. Kenney promised that he would personally place Bong on a transport in a day or two.

On this last day Bong, perhaps for the first time, learned a fact of war. Bong in his P-38 and Kenney in his B-17 proceeded to an airdrome at San Jose, Mindoro. Just as they landed and taxied to a parking area the sirens sounded. Colonel Gerald Richard Johnson, Bong's old group commander, led some P-38s to the attack.

When the Lightnings intercepted the Japanese formation, Johnson fired at the leader. The plane burst into flame instantly as Johnson turned away

". . . the formation was bounced by a single 'Hamp' . . ." *a later model of the Zero, the so-called clipped-wing variant of the maneuverable fighter. Also called* the "Hap," *the name was changed after General Henry* "Hap" *Arnold learned of this designation.*

(U. S. AIR FORCE)

to tackle another enemy aircraft. The action occurred almost directly over the field, so that Kenney and Bong watched in fascination.

As they watched, the Japanese pilot, unable to stand the flames, jumped from his plane. "The Jap pilot hit flat on the steel plank surface of the airdrome about a hundred feet from where Dick and I were standing. It was not a pretty sight. I watched for Bong's reaction. I had predicted a long while ago that if he ever found out that he was not shooting clay pigeons, I would have to take him out of combat. . . . He walked over to some bushes at the edge of the field and for the next five minutes was violently ill."

Kenney was certain more than ever that he was correct in taking Bong out of combat. McGuire, however, returned to the battle as soon as he knew that Bong had received his hero's welcome. Word came in on January 6, 1945; on the seventh McGuire was in the air again.

In the morning he took off in company with another experienced P-38 pilot (a Major Rittmayer of the Thirteenth Air Force) and two new pilots. To familiarize the green pilots, McGuire intended to make a quick sweep over a Japanese field on Negros Island, west of Leyte. The morning promised to be quiet, for as they flew along at about two thousand feet there seemed to be no Japanese air activity.

Unexpectedly the formation was bounced by a single "Hamp" (a late variant, the A6M3, of the Zero), which fastened itself to Rittmayer's tail, pouring fire into the P-38. McGuire reacted immediately and characteristically—he swept in to the rescue of the pilot in distress. To do this, however, he was forced to violate several of his own precepts for air combat. He had to turn the heavy P-38 tightly, and he had to do this at extremely low altitude—and with two heavy auxiliary fuel tanks attached to his wings.

McGuire apparently forgot about the wing tanks in the urgency of the moment, as he tipped the P-38 in a vertical bank to go to Rittmayer's aid. Ordinarily, since he was so skilled a pilot, he might have succeeded, but with the extra weight and resistance of the wing tanks it was not possible. In the tight turn the P-38 shuddered in mid-air for a moment, stalled, and then dropped straight to the ground. A massive explosion ripped out of the jungle. Meanwhile, the Hamp pilot persisted on the

other P-38, and in moments, Rittmayer joined McGuire in death. The Japanese pilot then slipped down among the hills of Los Negros and blended into the jungle and out of sight. The two new pilots returned to Leyte with the grim news.

The courageous Japanese pilot who single-handedly attacked the four-plane formation was, according to recent research, probably Shoichi Sugita. whose own victory tally placed him, by war's end, in the position of Japan's number two ace; he was therefore McGuire's Japanese counterpart. Sugita's score, however, was eighty, just twice that of Bong's.

Japanese aces, unlike those of the Allies and Germany, were not publicized; they were, in fact, as little known to their own countrymen as to the enemy. Partly this was because it was simply expected of them to serve the Emperor and if in so doing they shot down many enemy aircraft, so be it. Another reason for their scanty fame was simply class consciousness. Only the high officer class received due recognition; the non-commissioned officer or the skilled fighter who had come from the lower classes was not mentioned.

Nor were they looked after as in the fatherly manner of Kenney, "buccaneer" though he was supposed to be. Japanese pilots were expected to go until they died or dropped. Many flew in an exhausted, run-down state; many flew although seriously ill with malaria, dysentery, and other tropical diseases, or diseases caused by poor diet and fatigue.

One such remarkable pilot was Hiroyoshi Nishizawa, who, before he was killed while piloting a transport rather late in the war, shot down more than a hundred Allied planes. Nishizawa was Japan's top-scoring fighter pilot, although his name was not known during the war except to fellow pilots, who called him "the Devil." Sugita was second; the famed Saburo Sakai was third, with sixty-four victories. Other outstanding Japanese fighter pilots were Waturo Nakamichi (fifty-five victories), Naoshi Kanno (fifty-two), Yasuhiki Kuroe (fifty-one). Temei Akamatsu was one of the most fascinating airmen, for he was so totally un-Japanese in outlook. Like a throwback to the First World War, Akamatsu was an undisciplined advocate of wine and women and possibly song. His total score was fifty (he survived the war), which he shared with Kinsuke Muto and Toshio Ota.

These men fought under conditions of abuse and

A Japanese Nakajima L2D ("Tabby"), an obvious copy of the Douglas DC-3, such as carried Japanese ace Hiroyoshi Nishizawa to his death in the latter months of the war. (This Tabby was actually destroyed by Sergeant W. Tackett of Los Angeles from the top turret of a B-24 piloted by Captain Augustus V. Connery, East Providence, Rhode Island, while on a bombing mission over the Celebes.)

(U. S. AIR FORCE)

hardship which their commanders expected them to endure, in addition to being overwhelmed by a steady flow of fresh young pilots which the enemy sent against them. And these pilots flew better aircraft than the Japanese did toward the conclusion of the war.

But Bong was safely out of all that and happy in a new life; he had married Marjorie Vattendahl, the girl from Wisconsin, and he was working at the Lockheed plant in California, testing a new jet fighter, the P-80. Bong was still the American Ace of Aces; McGuire's score had been thirty-eight—and these would remain the two highest victory scores of the war.

Bong had made it, he had survived, a rare thing with top-scoring fighter pilots. But he could not elude the irony of endings; on the front page of the New York *Times* dated Tuesday, August 7, 1945, which carried the headline beginning "FIRST ATOMIC BOMB DROPPED ON JAPAN," there was another news item.

Just the day before, August 6, 1945, Richard Bong, aged twenty-five, died when the "Shooting Star" jet he was testing crashed and burned at Lockheed airport at Burbank. The concurrence of the two events, merging the atomic bomb and the jet aircraft, ended forever the kind of war that Richard Bong—and Neel Kearby, and Thomas Lynch, and Thomas McGuire, and, for that matter, George C. Kenney—had fought. History assured Bong his special place: he would be the American Ace of Aces forever and there would be no more rivals.

Approaching Guadalcanal, summer of 1942; in the foreground the Enterprise *and in the distance the* Saratoga. *Above, a Dauntless, with arrester hook down, is about to make a landing on the* Enterprise.
(NAVY DEPT., NATIONAL ARCHIVES)

BOOK II

Some Sailors—and
a Few Marines

3

THE ISLAND

THE military High Thinkers, with their penchant for simple but at the same time grandiloquent catchwords, called it Operation Watchtower. The directive, issued by the Joint Chiefs and dated July 2, 1942, ordered the South Pacific Force (Vice-Admiral Robert L. Ghormley commanding) to seize and occupy the "Santa Cruz Islands, Tulagi and adjacent positions" in the Solomon Islands chain. One of the "adjacent positions," not even mentioned in the directive, was an island named Guadalcanal.

The United States Marines, who took, held, and died on this pestilential island, coined their own word for the operation: Shoestring.

"Shoestring" was less grand than "Watchtower," but closer to the realities of the situation. Partially, the problem lay in the simple fact of inexperience in what was the first real offensive move in the war, and the first American amphibious operation since 1898. And it was made with less than adequate planning and equipment plus mixed emotions at high level. Ghormley was not too certain as to what his objectives were: Were we beginning on the road to Tokyo or merely stopping the Japanese before they became too well entrenched in the Solomons?

The entire operation had been conceived and set under way—inspired by the burgeoning airfield on Guadalcanal—in so great a hurry that Ghormley had little time to prepare for whatever it was he was supposed to accomplish. He was pessimistic, indeed, when he first began working on the project: there were no maps of the area, his amphibious forces had not yet arrived in the Pacific, and there was little intelligence on the disposition of the Japanese in the area. If Ghormley harbored doubts, Vice-Admiral Frank J. Fletcher, to whom he had delegated execution of the operation, did not like it at all—and said so. Fletcher as carrier commander was loath to expose his three precious carriers (the *Enterprise, Saratoga,* and *Wasp*) in an undertaking which he "opposed" and which he felt "sure . . . would be a failure."

He made it clear, in fact, at a meeting (not attended by Ghormley) before the assault, that he would not leave the carriers exposed while the Marines were being put ashore for more than two days. It was estimated that it would take five to complete the job. This would, of course, in turn, expose the Marines to attack by the Japanese. Fletcher's attitude, no doubt, could be attributed to the fact of his not seeing any point to the entire operation, and more subtly, to the fact that two carriers (the *Yorktown* and *Lexington*) had gone down under him; he did not wish to court further disasters.

But King, despite the objections of the Joint Chiefs, had initiated Watchtower, and it would go, as ordered, early in August 1942.

Bridge conference on the Wasp *with Dauntlesses spotted on flight deck. Hatless Commander D. F. Smith and steel-helmeted Captain Forrest Sherman, skipper of the carrier, attend while Rear Admiral Leigh Noyes receives report from Lieutenant Commander W. N. Beakley (back to camera). Operation Watchtower is under way.* (NAVY DEPT., NATIONAL ARCHIVES)

II

Guadalcanal stank—literally.

It was the effluvium of green decay that first told the sleepless Marines of the amphibious force in the early morning of August 7, 1942, that they had arrived off Red Beach. The smell of the place was evil and the consensus was best expressed by the Marine who was supposed to have said before the invasion began, "What do we want with a place nobody ever heard of before?" He was not alone,

for Ghormley back in Auckland at South Pacific Force headquarters and Fletcher aboard the *Saratoga,* a hundred miles south of Guadalcanal, struggled with the same question.

The initial aerial operations, following the pre-invasion softening up of the Guadalcanal-Tulagi-Gavutu area by the B-17s of Kenny's 11th Bombardment Group during the last week in July and early August, were the attacks by carrier planes upon the various proposed landing areas. Taking off from the *Enterprise, Wasp,* and *Saratoga* before sunrise, the Wildcats and Dauntlesses assembled in the still darkened sky about thirty miles west of Guadalcanal.

It was delicate, if nerve-racking work. In the darkness, although navigation lights were permitted, the usual mix-ups occurred. Fighters and bombers formed up, or squadrons intermixed as pilots mindful of collision gingerly tried to assemble with their own units. What unity had been achieved was suddenly dispersed when a sudden bright flash and explosion erupted under the rendezvous area. Scattering pilots were certain that two unfortunate planes had come together in the dark. Actually one of the Dauntless pilots had accidently dropped his bomb, which blew up on striking the water. By the time the fighters and scout bombers convened again, the invasion beaches—to the utter surprise of the Japanese—came under heavy fire from American naval big guns.

With the coming of first light, as the Marines clambered out of transports into landing craft offshore, the Wildcats and Dauntlesses swept over Beach Red (Guadalcanal) and Beach Blue (Tulagi, about twenty miles northeast of Florida Island). With very little opposition the carrier planes bombed and strafed the two landing areas, blasting buildings, vehicles, warehouses, gun emplacements, and, near Tulagi, a number of float planes moored offshore.

Shortly after 9 A.M. the Marines of the 1st Division began moving in—the landing at Guadalcanal proceeding "with the precision of a peacetime drill." It was not quite so in the vicinity of Beach Blue, where fifteen hundred Japanese fought, and most died, before the little islands of Tulagi, Gavutu, and Tanambogo could be declared secured.

The major problem on Guadalcanal at first seemed to be the accumulation of supplies on the beach. The Japanese troops (six hundred, not five thousand as Allied intelligence had assumed) fled inland, abandoning much of their own supplies. The laborers, who had been constructing the airstrip, inland and to the west of Beach Red, also faded into the jungle. Brigadier General Alexander A. Vandegrift, commanding the Marines, could not stop unloading troops in order to clear Guadalcanal's beaches of the clutter. By noon he realized that "smoothness" and "precision" were gone.

At twelve-thirty the first bombers from Rabaul arrived. Forty-five planes, bombers with fighter escort, of the 25th Koku Sentai opened up the Japanese counterattack. Navy F4Fs caught the initial wave over Florida Island, after Lieutenant Vincent DePoix of the *Enterprise* spotted them and led three other Wildcats into the attack.

Within minutes smoking Bettys dropped from the neat formations and Zeros whipped into the Wildcats. At the same time on the beaches, all unloading of transports was stopped and ships scurried about to afford as poor targets as possible for the bombers. Antiaircraft too came into action. The guns and the Navy fighters distracted the bombers, so there were no hits on the shipping as bombs dropped uselessly into Sealark Channel—a body of water between Florida and Guadalcanal which would become better known as "Iron Bottom Bay." During the early minutes of the first aerial battle over Guadalcanal Navy pilots deposited the initial metal into the bay in the form of Bettys and Zeros.

The first attack had been expected, thanks to an enterprising Australian coast watcher, the ex-planter Paul Mason, who saw the Bettys and Zeros flying over Buin on Bougainville, three hundred miles to the north of Guadalcanal. HQ radioed the message to Brisbane, which relayed it to Pearl Harbor, from which it was sent to the Solomons. But later in the afternoon another attack, this time by dive bombers, came in without advance warnings, and despite the Navy planes on combat air patrol, managed to strike the destroyer *Mugford*. While the ship did not sink, twenty-two men died in the bombing. *Saratoga* Wildcats all but annihilated the attackers, but the harm had been done.

The Japanese planes were as persistent as gnats, despite losses. (Of the fifty or so planes sent from Rabaul that day, about thirty were lost. It was in this first battle over Guadalcanal that Saburo Sakai was badly wounded and somehow managed to return to Rabaul in his Zero.) Some of the losses were those Vals which ran out of fuel on the way back. But a simple fact had emerged: the Japanese could be expected to fight hard for the "place nobody ever heard of before."

The reason lay in an unfinished airstrip on Guadalcanal. If the Japanese had expected to use it to strike at New Zealand and Australia-bound shipping, the Allies could employ it to hammer away at Rabaul.

D-Day, Guadalcanal, August 7, 1942. Bettys from Ra-baul skim the surface of Sealark Channel (Iron Bot-tom Bay) as antiaircraft bursts attempt to put them into the bay. (DEFENSE DEPT., MARINE CORPS)

While Guadalcanal remained quiet, the heavy fighting progressed across Sealark Channel. It was savage and bitter fighting, which, on land, gave the Americans the first shocking, acrid taste of the Japanese soldiers' lethal fighting style. For the time being, the Marines on Guadalcanal were spared this introduction. They gathered souvenirs abandoned by the Japanese, cursed the heat and the insects, and moved farther inland.

The aerial assault, despite the previous day's losses, continued on August 8. Early warning came via coast watcher Jack E. Read on Bougainville, who counted "Forty bombers heading yours." While the Navy Wildcats sought the expected attackers over Savo Island, in the channel between Guadalcanal and Florida, the Bettys dropped down to the water, skimmed in over Florida, and made for the ships.

As the Wildcats tangled with the Zeros overhead, the Bettys were met by a wall of antiaircraft from the ships in the channel. The bombers bore down upon the American ships, then flared one by one, cartwheeling in a pattern of flame before sinking into Iron Bottom Bay. At least a dozen Bettys went down in the wall of fire from the ships, but one released a torpedo, which struck the destroyer *Jarvis.* The *Jarvis* was caught by Japanese torpedo planes the following day as it made for Nouméa, New Caledonia, and sunk with all hands.

Another stricken Betty flew directly into the transport *George F. Elliott.* Although the troops had already left the ship, the supplies still in the hold burned and the *Elliott* was beyond salvation. The fire went out of control and the *Elliott* was scuttled at twilight—the first American contribution to the debris of Iron Bottom Bay.

The next morning there was much more. Vice-Admiral Gunichi Mikawa, after hastily assembling ships from Rabaul and Kavieng, raced to the Solomons to deal with the enemy. His orders opened with these words: "We will penetrate south of Savo Island and torpedo the enemy main force at Guadalcanal." And as he led his force of seven cruisers and a destroyer toward the island he wired the ships that "In the finest tradition of the Imperial Navy we shall engage the enemy in night battle. Every man is expected to do his best."

The weather and a series of American blunders

were with Mikawa. Fletcher, fearful lest his carriers be struck by Japanese planes or submarines, but using as an excuse that he was low on fuel (this was not true), withdrew the three carriers from Guadalcanal. This also withdrew Navy reconnaissance planes as well as the bombers and fighters which had been countering the Japanese. Although a search plane had spotted Mikawa's ships near Guadalcanal, its warning was neither properly understood nor distributed.

Early in the morning of August 9, 1942, Mikawa's cruisers began firing their deadly "Long Lance" torpedoes at the unsuspecting Allied ships. No one expected the Japanese, who all Americans were told and believed suffered from poor eyesight and could not see at night, to attack after one-thirty in the morning. Following a terrible night battle, the in-famous battle of Savo Island, the morning light found four heavy cruisers and a destroyer at the bottom of Iron Bottom Bay. More than a thousand men were dead and seven hundred wounded. Mikawa, unaware of his advantage, had slipped away before he did all the damage he might have done, but he had done enough.

By noon Rear Admiral Richmond Kelly Turner, who was in command of the ships of the amphibious force, withdrew his transports from the danger zone. With Fletcher gone and Turner gone, that left only sixteen thousand of Vandegrift's Marines, with only half their supplies, to wonder what the Japanese would try next. They had been furious in their air attacks, had wreaked havoc in the Battle of Savo Island. What would they try now?

The answer came with the initial run of the

The Ichiki detachment, transported to Guadalcanal by the newly instituted "Tokyo Express," has a rendez-vous with death and the U. S. Marines on the Tenaru River. Their major objective had been the airfield on Guadalcanal, which had fallen into American hands.
(DEFENSE DEPT., MARINE CORPS)

"Tokyo Express." The American ships having left Guadalcanal, the Japanese planes took to bombing the airfield being readied by the Marines. Submarines surfaced during the day to lob shells into it and destroyers stood offshore at night. Almost nightly "Washing Machine Charlie" flew down from Rabaul to keep the Marines from sleeping. The Japanese, certain there were only three thousand Americans on Guadalcanal (the actual number was closer to nineteen thousand), dispatched the Ichiki detachment to "quickly attack and destroy the enemy in the Solomons" in co-operation with the Japanese Imperial Navy.

The Ichiki detachment, commanded by Colonel Kiyanao Ichiki, was brought from Guam, to which it had been taken after the Midway fiasco. Instead of sailing home, as the detachment had been promised, it went instead to Truk, and by August 18, having been brought there by the Tokyo Express, began going ashore on Guadalcanal. Within two days the Ichiki detachment was ripped to pieces in a swift series of horrible battles. As Vandegrift reported, ". . . I have never heard or read of this kind of fighting. These people refuse to surrender. The wounded will wait until men come up to examine them . . . and blow themselves and the other fellow to pieces with a hand grenade."

Reinforcements for the "Cactus Air Force," Marine Wildcats at Henderson Field, Guadalcanal.
(DEFENSE DEPT., MARINE CORPS)

Having lost about eight hundred of his men in heedless slaughter (charging automatic weapons with bayonets), Ichiki had no other recourse but to join the honorable dead. After ripping his regimental colors to shreds, inundating them with oil, and setting them afire, Ichiki blew out his brains.

The pattern was established: if the Marines operated on a shoestring, the Japanese chose to use small rubber bands. From Rabaul the bands stretched dangerously; the Tokyo Express would bring in small, inadequate detachments under cover of night and the Imperial Navy would venture forth from time to time. But although they coveted Guadalcanal—especially its airfield—the Japanese High Command, with eyes elsewhere (New Guinea) was unwilling to pursue its course in the Solomons except fragmentally. In the ensuing hard six months, the Japanese and the Americans would learn a good deal about each other.

III

The day before the Battle of Tenaru River, which wiped out the Ichiki detachment, the first elements of what was called the "Cactus Air Force" landed upon Guadalcanal. On August 17, 1942, the Japanese field, taken over and completed by the Americans, was named Henderson Field, for the Marine dive bomber commander Major Lofton Henderson, who died at Midway. Cactus was the code name for Guadalcanal.

On August 20 the first Wildcats of Marine Aircraft Group (MAG) 23 began alighting on the strip at Lunga Point. These were nineteen new Grumman F4F-4s of Marine Fighter Squadron (VMF) 223, led by a lean Oklahoman, Captain John L. Smith. Along with the Wildcats came a dozen SBD-3s of Major Richard C. Mangrum's VMSB-232 (Marine Scout Bomber Squadron). The arrival of this tiny air force was greeted by the cheering Marines, who pitched in to change the hard-rubber tail wheels (for carrier deck landing) to pneumatic tires.

The next day Smith of Fighting 23 took four Wildcats out to strafe the remnants of the Ichiki detachment. While on patrol over Savo Island Smith sighted several Zeros and led his men in to the attack. The Zeros had the advantage of perhaps two thousand feet of altitude on the Wildcats, so Smith could do little else but turn the more rugged planes into the aggressors. A Zero flashed by without hitting Smith's plane; then another came in and Smith rolled and found the belly of the Zero in his sights. His mouth went dry, he later remembered, and his heart beat heavily as he squeezed the button. For an instant he watched the stitching of his guns travel along the underside of the Zero, which burst open and flamed. As Smith watched, the Japanese plane fell to the beach of Savo. He had killed his first enemy (the first of nineteen).

Turning back to the battle, Smith unhappily noticed that one Wildcat was missing. Searching, he led the two remaining planes to a formation of strangely gyrating and performing aircraft—but they were all Zeros. Why they insisted upon performing like so many Sunday afternoon pilots at an air show, Smith could not fathom. Perhaps they knew that the Wildcat could not dogfight with the Zero; at the same time they wasted the precious fuel for the long return flight to Rabaul—if they ever got there.

Smith led the two pilots back to Henderson, where they saw the fourth Wildcat. Technical Sergeant John D. Lindley's F4F had been hit in the Zero attack and he made for the landing strip, where he crash-landed. Emerging oil-soaked from the cockpit, Lindley collapsed to the ground. He was not

John L. Smith, USMC, commander of the first squadron of fighters to arrive at Guadalcanal. Smith survived the months of hard fighting over the Solomons (for which he received the Medal of Honor), later became an instructor. (DEFENSE DEPT., MARINE CORPS)

seriously hurt and eventually returned to the battle. But his plane was out for the time being.

Fighting 23 had had its first encounter with the dreaded Zero, and although they lost a plane, they had not lost a man. And Captain Smith had actually scored against a Zero. The myth of the invincible Zero was nearing its bitter end.

But the little Cactus Air Force grew slightly. On August 22 the 67th Fighter Squadron, commanded by Captain Dale Brannon, flew up with five Army P-400s (the inferior export P-39, which pilots called "Klunkers"). Two days later an unexpected increment, eleven SBDs, orphans on the wing, flew from the stricken *Enterprise*. These were the Dauntlesses of "Flight 300" led by Lieutenant Turner Caldwell, which, unable to land on the thrice-hit deck of the *Enterprise* during the Battle of the Eastern Solomons, were forced to seek haven at Henderson Field. Immediately drafted into the

Bell P-39s, which in its export version was designated P-400 (originally intended for Britain but repossessed by the Army after Pearl Harbor). Although disparagingly called "Klunkers" by Air Force pilots, the planes served with distinction in the Cactus Air Force. Here they are mud-mired on Henderson.

(U. S. AIR FORCE)

Cactus Air Force, these strays from the *Enterprise* would spend the next month on Guadalcanal.

Thus the battle for Guadalcanal took on its own peculiar forms: on land, at sea, and in the air, with Henderson Field at the focus of action. Emphasis might shift from one aspect of the fighting to the other when the fighting on land erupted bloodily; and then it might shift to the sea (such as the ill-starred Battle of Savo Island). The aerial fighting was generally on a small scale because both forces operated under their individual handicaps—the Marines and their small units, lack of spare parts, minimal fuel supply, and the problem of the weather and climate.

The Japanese had access to a supply of replacement aircraft (which were brought into Rabaul from the homeland, Tinian, Truk, and other outposts). These planes and the new pilots were then tossed away in piecemeal, wasteful attempts. Both aircraft and men were pressed beyond endurance and both were consumed with abandon.

When both sea and air battle combined, the results were more decisive than the prodigal thrusts from Rabaul. Such was the Battle of the Eastern

Solomons (August 24–25, 1942). In this engagement, primarily a battle of carrier forces, land-based Marine aircraft participated in their first major air battle in the Solomons.

Yamamoto had assigned a formidable armada of carriers, battleships, and cruisers to protect four transports of the Tokyo Express carrying fifteen hundred troops to Guadalcanal. The striking force, under Nagumo, somewhat recovered from Midway, was based upon the heavy carriers *Shokaku* and *Zuikaku;* the light carrier *Ryujo* was assigned to a diversionary group under Rear Admiral Chuichi Hara, whose task it was to draw American attention away from Rear Admiral Raizo Tanaka's transports and the big carriers.

When word came in from coast watchers and reconnaissance planes of the presence of large Japanese naval forces proceeding toward Guadalcanal, Admiral Ghormley ordered Fletcher's three carriers north to cover the sea approaches to Guadalcanal. Ever since Fletcher had pulled away from Guadalcanal he had patrolled in the seas to the south of the Solomons. By dawn of August 23 the *Enterprise, Saratoga,* and *Wasp* lay east of Malaita Island (about 150 miles east of Henderson Field).

August 22 and 23 the two fleets feinted gingerly in unfavorable weather (unfavorable, that is, for search planes), neither actually finding the other although both Japanese and Americans knew of

A Marine Wildcat takes off to meet an oncoming Japanese bomber force. Henderson was either soaked in mud or choked with dust, neither of which was salutary for engines or aircraft.

(DEFENSE DEPT., MARINE CORPS)

one another's presence. Fletcher, misinformed by his intelligence that the Japanese fleet still lay far to the north and thus not expecting action, sent the *Wasp,* with its screen, off to refuel. This left the *Saratoga* and *Enterprise* aircraft plus the tatterdemalions of the Cactus Air Force to take on Yamamoto's forces.

As the *Wasp* pulled away to the south, Yamamoto ordered Vice-Admiral Nobutake Kondo, commanding the Guadalcanal supporting force, to press on with the attack.

Shortly after nine o'clock on the morning of August 24 an American Catalina on patrol spotted a Japanese carrier, just about 200 miles north of Malaita—and about 280 miles from Fletcher's remaining carriers. It was the *Ryujo* on its mission of diverting Fletcher away from the other two Japanese carriers and the landing forces approaching Guadalcanal.

While the ruse worked—Fletcher dispatched bombers and torpedo planes from the *Saratoga* and *Enterprise*—the cost was rather excessive for the inconsiderable *Ryujo.* After dodging the *Enterprise* Avengers and Dauntlesses, it was struck by planes from the *Saratoga* and sunk. Meanwhile, the fifteen bombers and dozen fighters which the *Ryujo* had launched earlier had tangled with Smith's Fighting 23 on the way to attack Henderson Field.

Not one of the Japanese planes reached Guadalcanal. The Wildcats intercepted the Japanese formation and destroyed sixteen enemy aircraft—six of which were Zeros. One of Smith's few veterans of VMF-223—a veteran, in fact, of Midway—Captain Marion Carl knocked down two Kates and a Zero himself. Other Fighting 23 members, Lieutenants Zennith A. Pond and Kenneth D. Frazier and Gunner Henry B. Hamilton, each shot down two of the attackers. The surviving Kates and Zeros, driven off by the Wildcats, returned to the *Ryujo,* only to find a crazily listing, careening, and burning carrier. The planes were ordered to fly on to the Japanese field at Buka near Bougainville to the north.

The Marines of Fighting 23 chipped away further at the myth of the Zero in the opening fight of the Battle of the Eastern Solomons. But not without cost to them, for the squadron suffered its first serious losses that day. Fred Gutt, noted for his sardonic humor, was seriously wounded; Roy Corry,

The Zero, specifically the "Zeke 52," the mythical fighter of the early months of the Pacific war, but which the Marines, especially of Smith's "Fighting 23," found vulnerable. A beautifully designed, nimble aircraft, the Zero was susceptible to the heavy-gunned American planes. Its pilots were unprotected by armored cockpits and it burned easily.

(U. S. AIR FORCE)

the gunnery officer—also, like Carl, a Midway veteran and who had given Smith cause for concern on the ship coming over because he brooded about his chances of death in the air—was lost. The last seen of him was when he dived into a swarm of Zeros. The first to go, however, had been a youngster named Bailey who had married just the day before he joined VMF-223. His Wildcat was last seen afire as it splashed into the sea.

The *Ryujo* and its aircraft having been attended to, there still remained the *Shokaku* and *Zuikaku,* whose special targets were the American carriers. Almost simultaneously the two carrier captains, Fletcher and Nagumo, became aware of each other's presence when their respective search planes came upon carriers. This was Nagumo's desired moment; he ordered the aircraft launched, the first wave, consisting of sixty-seven planes led by Lieutenant Commander Mamoru Seki, which raced for the spot where an American carrier had been sighted. A second wave, launched less than an hour later and consisting of forty-eight planes, was led astray by a navigational error and never found the American carriers.

Seki's Kates, Vals, and Zeros, however, found the *Enterprise.* As soon as "bogies" were discovered on the radarscopes of the two American carriers, now about ten miles apart, the air above them filled with more than fifty Wildcats. Lieutenant A. O. Vorse, leading a section of four F4Fs from the *Saratoga,* was the first to sight the Japanese planes —two groups of bombers, shepherded above and below by fighters.

With a shout of "Tally Ho!" Vorse pointed the four Wildcats at the bombers, still about ten thousand feet higher than the American planes. Zeros dropped down to intercept, but the Wildcats, straining at full throttle, continued to climb above the Zero's top altitude. Now with the advantage of altitude, Vorse led a screaming attack upon the Japanese bombers. But again the Zeros darted in to disrupt the run on the bombers, and in the ensuing dogfight three Zeros and what appeared to be an Me-109 fell burning into the sea. Out of ammunition and low on fuel, the four Wildcats returned to the *Saratoga,* except for Vorse, who had to land in the water—he did not have enough fuel to make it all the way. A destroyer swept by to pick him up.

But the bombers continued coming in. Some had dropped very low to avoid radar, but four Wildcats, the section of Ensign G. W. Brooks, had been dispatched by the fighter director of the *Enterprise* to investigate a curious echo on the radarscope. Sixty miles from the carrier Brooks and his section found eleven bombers, Vals and Kates—but without Zeros —heading for the *Enterprise.* Brooks's first burst destroyed a Val, and as he turned away, a Kate came into his sights. Another quick burst and the bomber splashed wing over wing across the water. Within minutes four other bombers, victims of the other members of Brooks's section, fell into the sea, three of them shot down. One Val, its pilot rattled by the attack, simply flew into the water. The five survivors turned tail and fled.

Above the *Enterprise,* too, the battle raged, and burning aircraft—American as well as Japanese— fell into the Pacific. With all its fighters air-borne and its bombers aloft, the *Enterprise* waited. Men on deck squinted into the sunny yet cloud-flecked sky, smeared by the smoke of falling aircraft. Crews at their battle stations manned their 20-millimeters. About twenty-five miles away from the *Enterprise,* Seki fired a signal flare. The Zeros had climbed to

engage the Wildcats, the Kates descended to near water level for torpedo attacks, and the Vals, dividing into small groups, prepared for dive attacks.

Around twelve minutes after five in the afternoon, the first Val tipped on its nose and dropped toward the *Enterprise.* Even while it was still out of range a nervous 20-millimeter gunner indicated its approach with his tracers. In seconds other guns, from the carrier itself and from its escort, the *North Carolina,* joined in on the Val. Soon other bombers followed the Val; the Japanese pilots felt that they were diving into "a wall of fire."

But they came on nonetheless, despite the heavy antiaircraft fire and the Wildcats. Within two minutes of the opening of the attack the *Enterprise* took its first bomb of the war. It struck the aft elevator and cut through three decks before detonating. The explosion whipped the *Enterprise,* throwing men in the forward section to the deck, blasting men from their gun positions, tossing them like rag dolls across the decks. Below, where the bomb had burst, more than thirty men lay dead.

Within seconds a second bomb burst, five yards from where the first had hit. In a searing flash, men suddenly vanished from the earth. The great carrier, spouting black smoke, listed; a quarter of its guns were out of action and more than seventy men dead. But repair parties went to work immediately attending to dozens of injured, and began to clear the damaged area and to contain the fires.

Even while this went on a third bomb fell onto the flight deck. Less effective than the first two bombs, the third, however, ripped a ten-foot hole out of the flight deck and knocked an elevator out of operation.

Suddenly, after about four minutes of concentrated havoc, the last of Seki's bombers, a Val, hugging the water raced for its own carrier.

The listing, burning *Enterprise,* though in serious trouble, was not in danger. Even while the damage-repair crews worked, the great ship continued to make speed and even informed the concerned men aboard the *North Carolina* that it "required no assistance." Within an hour after the last bomb had struck, the *Enterprise* was able to turn into the wind to land its aircraft, all except Turner Caldwell's fuel-depleted Flight 300, which landed at Henderson Field (to join the Cactus Air Force).

The *Saratoga* escaped attack, and although two

The third bomb striking the Enterprise, *putting the elevator out of operation and killing Navy photographer*

Robert Frederick Read. Following the Battle of the Eastern Solomons, the Enterprise *was under repair for two months.* (NAVY DEPT., NATIONAL ARCHIVES)

heavy Japanese carriers were found, they too escaped serious damage (the *Zuikaku* received one bomb on the flight deck). Returning Japanese pilots gleefully reported sinking the *Hornet,* Doolittle's "Shangri-La," and thus avenging the insult to the Emperor. It was, of course, the *Enterprise,* not the *Hornet,* and it was not sunk, but would be out of battle for two months while being repaired at Pearl Harbor.

The carrier battle was over on the first day; both Fletcher and Nagumo gingerly husbanded their carrier strength. As the day came to a close, five Avengers and two Dauntlesses, led by Lieutenant

Harold Larsen of the *Saratoga,* were sent out to do something about Kondo's advance force heading for Guadalcanal. The handful of planes attacked and sent the seaplane carrier *Chitose* back to Truk with a thirty-degree list, the loss of the port engine, a fire aboard, and casualties. Kondo continued looking for Fletcher, but by midnight gave up the search.

But "Tenacious" Tanaka, the brilliant overseer of the Tokyo Express, continued on for Guadalcanal with his troop-laden transports. While the carriers and fighting ships had been battling to the east of the Solomons, Tanaka had been coming in from the north. On the morning of August 25, Tanaka's ships

"You never had it so good"—*Marine camp on Guadalcanal during the rainy season.*

were discovered and Mangrum's Dauntlesses of VMSB-232 and the mixed bag of strays of the *Enterprise,* Flight 300, took off to stop the Japanese.

Before they had found the ships, however, Smith had to turn back his protective Wildcats, at the end of their fuel for the trip out. The Henderson Field bombers, meanwhile, continued their search. Suddenly, as if they had materialized out of the mist, there were the ships: the cruiser *Jintsu,* Tanaka's flagship, plus eight destroyers and the transports.

The Marine and Navy bombers struck. Lieutenant Lawrence Baldinus, of VMSB-232, neatly placed a bomb on the deck of the *Jintsu,* just forward of the bridge and between the two forward turrets. In a

reverberating flash, the ship leaped in the water. Tanaka was knocked unconscious as plates buckled, bulkheads were sprung, communications went out, and the forward ammunition lockers flooded. Tanaka, when he came to, realized his flagship was finished as a warship for the time being. He transferred his flag to the destroyer *Kagero* and ordered the *Jintsu* to return to Truk.

Having barely taken up his new post, Tanaka saw Ensign Christian Fink of Flight 300 place a thousand-pound bomb into the heavily loaded transport *Kinryu Maru.* He immediately ordered the destroyers *Mutsuki* and *Yayoi* to run alongside the stricken transport, glowing with heat, to take off survivors.

The American dive bombers, having expended their bombs, circled the scene of damage—the *Jintsu* limping away and the *Kinryu Maru* (which was later sunk) burning furiously—and returned to Henderson. Tanaka then felt he could apply himself better to the problems at hand. But no sooner had the Dauntlesses become specks in the south than high overhead appeared a formation of eight Flying Fortresses. This was not so distressing to Tanaka; as the antiaircraft batteries opened up on these planes, from Colonel LaVerne Saunder's 11th Bombardment Group based in the New Hebrides, Tanaka took some consolation in the fact that the high-flying heavy bombers had never hit a ship, despite American claims to the contrary.

A pattern of five-hundred-pound bombs tumbled from the open bomb bays and before Tanaka's horrified eyes the *Mutsuki* erupted in a series of three flashes and sank. Shortly after, around noon August 25, 1942, Tanaka was ordered to retire to the Shortland Islands, one of the smaller Solomon groups, south of Bougainville. The first major attempt by the Japanese to reinforce Guadalcanal had failed; it had cost them the *Ryujo,* ninety aircraft, and hundreds of men. American losses amounted to seventeen planes and the services of the injured *Enterprise* for several weeks. If the battle of the carriers had not been truly decisive, at least the full contingent of reinforcements had not been landed on Guadalcanal.

IV

That Marine and Navy morale was high could not be attributed to conditions at Henderson Field. For all its blood-soaked significance, Henderson was no pleasure drome. "Henderson Field," Robert Sherrod wrote, "was a bowl of black dust which fouled airplane engines or it was a quagmire of black mud. . . ." Maintenance of the few aircraft was formidable because of the dust and mud; then too there was the humidity. The oil that prevented gun barrels from rusting on the ground caused them to freeze up at fighting altitude.

Ground crews therefore had as tough a time as the airmen. All shared the miseries of climate and the shortage of fresh food (captured Japanese rice was eaten, but only after the careful removal of worms). Malaria and dysentery were common and

so was nagging fatigue. There was no rest at night thanks to "Washing Machine Charlie" or "Louie the Louse," who either dropped random bombs or lighted up the Marine areas with flares so that Tanaka's ships could shell the field and the Marine positions around it.

Yet there was a dash to the style of the pilots of the Cactus Air Force. They became familiar, when photographs came out of the Solomons, in their informal flight clothes all but invariably topped with a blue baseball cap—popular because the visor protected the eyes from the blinding sun. But living and fighting operations took their toll and the problem of reinforcement and supply became critical.

During the day supplies could be brought in by American ships—provided they eluded Japanese submarines and planes. When night fell the big ships raced away from Guadalcanal and the smaller vessels slipped into Tulagi; the land-based Marines dug in. All awaited the arrival of the Tokyo Express, which arrived to land reinforcements and to bring in supplies while its destroyer escort shelled the American positions. Thus, piecemeal, each side kept the fighting going but neither was able to swing the balance.

But piece by piece the American buildup continued at what seemed a piddling pace to those Marines on Guadalcanal. Clearly the Japanese intended to take back Henderson Field, and so it became essential to hold the island. At the end of August the rest of MAG-23 joined its forward echelons—these were Major Robert E. Galer's VMF-224 (with nineteen Wildcats) and Major Leo R. Smith's VMSB-231 (twelve Dauntlesses). At the same time, however, almost twice as many planes were flown in to reinforce Rabaul. The situation remained generally as before: shoestring and rubber band. But standing resolutely between the proper reinforcement by the Japanese of the Guadalcanal forces were the shoestring Marines, the bombers and fighters of Kenney's Fifth Air Force, and the few B-17s and P-39s of those groups that would one day be unified into the Thirteenth Air Force.

Vice-Admiral John S. McCain, commander of all air operations in the South Pacific, stated the facts when he informed Nimitz that "Guadalcanal can be consolidated, expanded and exploited to the enemy's mortal hurt, the reverse is true if we lose Guadalcanal and if reinforcement required is not available Guadalcanal cannot be supplied and cannot be held."

Plenty of action soon blooded the newly arrived Fighting 24 and squadron commander Galer himself opened his string of victories with a double. The veterans of Fighting 23 joined with the new men on missions in order to give them the benefit of their experience.

John Smith continued as his squadron's leading ace with his closest competitor for that position being Marion Carl. But even the veterans could lose a battle, and on September 14, 1942 (while on land the Marines fought at Bloody Ridge to hold Henderson from a heavy attack) Carl's Wildcat was shot into the sea. Carl checked his parachute and took to the air himself. Landing in the water, he swam to shore, where he met one Corporal Eroni, one of the local scouts in the service of Martin Clemens, the Australian coast watcher.

It took Carl and Eroni five days to return to Henderson Field, during which time the colorful and likable pilot was mourned by his squadron mates. He arrived a gaunt, unshaven tall man in dirty khakis at the headquarters of the commander of the 1st Marine Air Wing (1st MAW), Brigadier General Roy S. Geiger. The latter had only recently arrived in Guadalcanal himself to organize operations. His headquarters had been established only two weeks previously in a wooden shack, called "the Pagoda" by the men, about two hundred yards from the Henderson runway—called "the Bull's-eye."

When Carl reported to Geiger the latter was visibly pleased that the man given up for lost had returned. So was Smith, who happened to be in the Pagoda. After relating his adventures with Eroni and the wheezy little launch that had brought him back, Carl—as had the aces in New Guinea—wondered about his score as compared with Smith's.

"Well," Geiger told him, "Smitty has run his score up to fourteen during the five days you were away. That puts you only three behind. What can we do about it?"

"Goddammit, General," Carl retorted, "ground him for five days!"

Thus did the double-edged sword of attrition oscillate from one crisis to the other. Three days before Marion Carl went temporarily missing Cactus Air Force received an unexpected reinforcement: twenty-four Wildcats of VF-5 (Lieutenant Com-

Robert E. Galer, commander of Marine Fighting 24 of Guadalcanal, thirteenth-scoring ace of the Marine Corps and Medal of Honor recipient.

(DEFENSE DEPT., MARINE CORPS)

mander Leroy C. Simpler commanding), rendered homeless after the torpedoing of the *Saratoga* by Japanese submarine I-26. While the carrier put into Pearl Harbor, joining the *Enterprise,* there also undergoing repair, its airmen spent nearly ten days twiddling their thumbs at Espiritu Santo in the New Hebrides. By September 11, 1942, they had arrived at Henderson in time for the heavy battling around the airfield.

Although Admiral Ghormley had consistently refused to permit carrier-based aircraft to operate from Guadalcanal (except the *Enterprise*'s Flight 300, which had no other place to go), he dispatched Simpler's Wildcats to Henderson's attrition center. Obviously something was brewing—and it was, for the Japanese were determined to seize Henderson Field.

The operational toll at Henderson because of primitive repair facilities and fatigued pilots was

Marion E. Carl of Hubbard, Oregon, and a top-scoring ace of Fighting 23. (DEFENSE DEPT., MARINE CORPS)

high. On one day in September, for example, eight planes crashed during takeoff. Two were put together again but the remaining half dozen were dragged off to the plane bone yard to be cannibalized for parts. One fighter pilot, it was reported, looked at the growing junk heap and said to another, "At this rate we can whip ourselves without any assistance from the Japs."

Bombing attacks were intensified, Japanese destroyers shelled Marine positions, and Major General Kiyotaki Kawaguchi arrived, via the Tokyo Express, in the evening of the same day the Saratoga had been hit, to organize the taking of Henderson. These plans were most thorough, for they embraced even the surrender ceremonies in which the Americans were expected to participate in the role of the vanquished.

Meanwhile, with the pickup in the activity of the Tokyo Express, a concentration of naval forces at

Truk-Palau, and additional aircraft flown into Rabaul noted, all efforts were made to reinforce the Marines at Guadalcanal. When Kawaguchi struck on September 12 one battalion, led by Lieutenant Colonel Kusukichi Watanabe, was expected "to dash through to the airfield." The Marines, expecting something, took a different view. Like the Ichiki detachment, Kawaguchi's force, which fought furiously, was chopped to pieces by the Marines. Further, Kawaguchi's men came under various air attacks, one of the worst being the noonday (September 12) visit by more than two dozen Bettys with Zero escort, which mistakenly bombed and strafed Kawaguchi's rear echelon at Tasimboko on the north coast.

Even the Klunkers, the three remaining airworthy 67th Squadron P-400s, came in low during the final phase of the Battle of Bloody Ridge to end all Japanese hopes of making the dash to Henderson Field.

The fighting was hard and the Marines suffered 59 dead (to the Japanese toll of 708), but despite the clear-cut victory on land, there was a disaster at sea.

On September 15, the day following the Battle of Bloody Ridge, the *Hornet* and *Wasp*, the two remaining carriers in the Pacific, had been called to escort six transports carrying the 7th Marines to Guadalcanal. While moving into the waters of the Coral Sea known as "Torpedo Junction" (between Espiritu Santo and Guadalcanal), the carriers came under submarine attack. The battleship *North Carolina* was hit by a torpedo; so was the destroyer *O'Brien*. Although the *North Carolina* remained afloat and returned to Espiritu Santo, the *O'Brien*, after making temporary repairs, split in two on its way to the United States.

The *Hornet* eluded the Japanese "fish" but three twenty-one-inch torpedoes ripped into the *Wasp* and it sank, a burning mass of junk. That left only the *Hornet* against Nagumo's large carriers, the *Shokaku* and *Zuikaku*, and the light carriers *Zuiho* and *Junyo*. This was an unhealthy imbalance of naval power in the Pacific and it did not bode well for the Marines and Navy and Army men on Guadalcanal.

The only slight brightness was the additional Navy aircraft that, deckless because of the loss of carriers, bolstered up the always tattered Cactus Air Force. "What saved Guadalcanal," Brigadier General Ross

The Wasp, *torpedoed en route to Guadalçanal, before it sank on September 15, 1942.*

(NAVY DEPT., NATIONAL ARCHIVES)

E. Rowell, commander of the Marine Pacific Air Wings, commented, "was the loss of so many carriers." On October 1, 1942, General Geiger had a total of fifty-eight operational aircraft (Wildcats, Dauntlesses, Avengers, and the usual three Klunkers) on Guadalcanal. But at Rabaul the Japanese had about three times this number.

And the Japanese remained resolute in their plans to take Guadalcanal. Lieutenant General Harukichi Hyakutake, commander of the Seventeenth Army at Rabaul, had his own timetable to keep. His major project was the taking of Port Moresby, but before that he wished to recapture Guadalcanal by October 21. After the disasters of the Ichiki detachment and the Kawaguchi force,

however inexplicable, Hyakutake proposed to lead the recapture himself. As additional insurance he built his force around two tough divisions, veterans of the fighting in the Philippines, Java, and other conquered areas. These units, the 2nd (Sendei) and 38th Divisions, were equipped with heavy artillery and tanks, neither of which Ichiki nor Kawaguchi had had. At the same time the aircraft strength at Rabaul was raised to 180; a bomber base was established at Buka in the northern Solomons and fighters could be accommodated at Buin on Bougainville. Even the generally unsympathetic Imperial Navy co-operated with the promise of such great battleships as the *Haruna, Kongo, Hiei,* and *Kirishima.* The Tokyo Express was in fine shape.

Chief aerial contenders in the critical phase of the war in the Pacific. Straddling the center fold near top, is the Douglas C-47 (the DC-3 of civil life), in battle dress, which served in all war theaters as a freighter and troop transport and was used to transport 7,000 Allied troops across the Owen Stanley Mountains in New Guinea. Continuing counterclockwise: a Mitsubishi A6M2 "Zero" fighter in the markings of Saburo Sakai, based at Lae, New Guinea, in the summer of 1942; Douglas A-20 *Havoc* which was widely used as a deadly skip-bomber by Kenney's Fifth Air

Force; the Grumman F6F *Hellcat,* the plane designed specifically to deal with the "Zero;" Mitsubishi G4M "Betty," land-based Navy medium bomber, which ranged over the Pacific; Lockheed P-38J *Lightning* as flown by Richard Bong of the 49th Fighter Group, Fifth Air Force; Grumman TBF (actually an Eastern Aircraft TBM, manufactured by General Motors) *Avenger,* which fared so badly at the Battle of Midway but exceedingly well in the later battles; Grumman F4F *Wildcat,* the standard Navy fighter at the war's opening.

Joseph A. Phelan

By the time Hyakutake himself arrived by the nightly express he had around twenty thousand (perhaps several thousands more; precise figures were not maintained during these tense days) troops awaiting the word to go. On this October 9 Hyakutake, the soul of efficiency, had a good idea of which spot was to be selected for the surrender of General Vandegrift.

On this same day twenty Wildcats of MAG-14 arrived (making the total forty-six fighters); the planes were led in by Major Leonard K. Davis. These were the aircraft of VMF-121, a squadron whose executive officer was Captain Joseph J. Foss. Smith's veteran VMF-223 had by this time become depleted with six pilots killed and six wounded. Eight, among them Smith himself, survived. Smith, with a score of 19, was the squadron's ace, and Marion Carl was second with a total of 16. But the contribution of Fighting 23 did not lay in numbers (the squadron total was 111½), but in the day-to-day fighting against odds for nearly two months. For his part John L. Smith was awarded the Medal of Honor and returned to the United States to train future Marine fighter pilots.

Richard Mangrum, who led the first of the Dauntless squadrons (VMSB-232), like Smith, survived although the squadron had suffered eleven killed (seven of whom were pilots) and five wounded (four of these being pilots); the rest of the squadron had to be evacuated by air for hospitalization. Only Mangrum was able to leave under his own power.

Flight 300 of the *Enterprise* had been used up in the battling and its last crew members were shipped out to return to their carrier by late September. The weight of the bombing effort out of Henderson devolved upon Major Gordon A. Bell's VMSB-141, which began arriving on September 23 and which by October 6 could muster twenty-one pilots, and upon Leo Smith's depleted VMSB-231 and other strays which had come in from the south.

Joseph Foss got his first Zero on October 13, 1942, during an afternoon raid by Japanese bombers and Zeros. It was this day which the Japanese selected to open their final seizure of Guadalcanal, which Hyakutake told his troops would "truly decided the fate of the entire Pacific."

The first of the Japanese bombers, coming over just after noon, holed the runway at Henderson and a nearby strip, Fighter 1. Even more irreparable harm was done when five thousand gallons of aviation fuel went up in smoke. More bombers came over about an hour later and again Henderson was worked over. Because both raids had come without advance warning there was little opportunity for interception, except for a couple of Zeros, one of them shot down by Foss.

Just before these raids the first Army troops, the "Americal Division" (164th Infantry Regiment), had debarked to be treated to the typical atmosphere of Guadalcanal. Nighttime brought even more of the same. To the Marines' surprise, just after six o'clock in the evening shells began falling on Henderson. There were no Japanese ships offshore. This was "Pistol Pete," one of the heavy artillery guns which had been brought in on the Tokyo Express only two nights before.

But that was only the preliminary to the evening's diversion. From time to time Pistol Pete would lob one over, just to keep everyone on their toes, and nerves' edge, and then in the middle of the night Louie the Louse flew over and planted three flares across Henderson Field, a red one at one end, white in the middle, and blue at the other end. For the next hour and a half the *Haruna* and the *Kongo*

Marines extinguish a burning Wildcat at Henderson Field after a Japanese bombing raid.

(DEFENSE DEPT., MARINE CORPS)

laid more than nine hundred fourteen-inch shells into the Henderson area, ripping up the steel matting of the runways, damaging planes, and killing men. It was a nightmare, literally, of flame, explosion, and terror. As Tanaka observed he found that "the whole spectacle [made] the Ryogoku fireworks display seem like mere child's play. The night's pitch dark was transformed by fire into the brightness of day. Spontaneous cries and shouts of excitement ran throughout our ships."

This exhilaration was not echoed ashore. When the Marines and soldiers finally crawled from their foxholes, the destruction their bleary eyes took in was disheartening. To begin with, forty-one men were dead, five of them pilots; one of the latter was Major Gordon Bell, only recently arrived with his replacement Dauntlesses. General Geiger, who had dived into shelter knowing he had thirty-nine Dauntlesses to dispatch against the Japanese, found upon emerging that only four were still flyable. Sixteen of his forty Wildcats were wrecks and all of the remaining ones required repairs. Two Flying Fortresses, of eight which had arrived from Espiritu Santo, were destroyed. The surviving six got away from Henderson as soon as possible, some on less than full power.

About the only damage that no one regretted was

a direct hit upon a ration dump which deposited bits and pieces of Spam in every direction for a half mile. And since the airfield was the center of attention, General Geiger's Pagoda was also hit. This structure, which afforded the Japanese a good aiming point, was bulldozed to the ground, and the Marine aviation commander moved his headquarters to the eastern end of Henderson Field.

And so it went on: savage fighting in the jungle around Henderson, bombardment by night and day, as each contender attempted to reinforce their forces on the island. This made for what Samuel Eliot Morison called "a curious tactical situation . . . : a virtual exchange of sea mastery every twelve hours." It was like some mad changing of the guard, with the Japanese in control at night and the Americans by day. But Hyakutake, with the aid of Yamamoto, hoped to change all that once and for all.

The night following "the Night," as the Marines called it, the Japanese ships returned, this time in the form of a couple of cruisers, which laced the Henderson area with nearly eight hundred eight-inch shells to cover the landing of more reinforcements. By dawn of the next day, October 15, the Japanese believed that Henderson had been pretty well taken care of—and they were not far from wrong. In the morning an American search plane came upon five Japanese transports, standing off Tassafaronga (about ten miles west of Henderson on the north coast of Guadalcanal) rather discon-

Bombed-up Dauntlesses over Guadalcanal head for their targets—ships of the Tokyo Express.

(DEFENSE DEPT., MARINE CORPS)

A Consolidated PBY "Catalina," a patrol bomber that Marine Major "Mad Jack" Cram converted (for one battle) into a dive bomber.

(CONVAIR/GENERAL DYNAMICS)

certingly unloading troops and supplies in broad daylight.

Geiger found he had little with which to contest this affront. Only three Dauntlesses were in condition to get off the ground, and only one actually did. The other two cracked up while attempting to get off the pocked Henderson runway. But single attacks could accomplish very little, especially when the Zeros could come down from Bougainville to circle over the transports. But as the day progressed, ground crew men patched up the aircraft and found some long-forgotten supplies of fuel hidden in the swamps around the airfield; they siphoned this fuel into whatever planes could be mustered for disputing with the Japanese their bold attempt to take over during the American daylight period of sea mastery.

By ten in the morning, three hours after the first single-plane attacks, a dozen Dauntlesses were ready to fly. Wildcats, Klunkers (P-400s), and even a single Catalina went out to raze the transports' rendezvous area. Major Jack Cram, the pilot of the Catalina, *Blue Goose,* General Geiger's personal aircraft, took off with two two-thousand-pound torpedoes slung under the Catalina's wing. He had arrived from Espiritu Santo with the torpedoes, but

found there were no Avengers in condition to de-
liver them. Although no PBY had ever made a daylight torpedo run before, Cram, by dint of vocal
power, obtained permission to drop the fish. Cram,
who earned the nickname of "Mad Jack" on this
mission, took off in company with a mixed flight of
Dauntlesses and Wildcats. Counting his slow Catalina, the American formation consisted of twenty-
one planes. Over the Japanese transports milled about
thirty Zeros.

As the Dauntlesses raced in for their attacks,
Cram set the Catalina on its own, near-dawdling
bomb run. The big plane soon came under antiaircraft fire from the ships (one hit sheared off
the plane's navigation hatch). Cram bore down on
one of the transports and released the torpedoes,
both of which tore into the side of one of the
transports, ripping it open.

Mad Jack Cram, though successful in his unorthodox mission, was now in plenty of trouble.
Several Zeros, upon realizing what the pilot of the
Catalina had been up to, peeled out of the fighting
above and began devoting full attention to the *Blue
Goose*. Having already dived the Catalina beyond
its normal safe speed, Cram tested the groaning
airframe and wing even more in attempting to evade
the Zeros. Although he managed to keep his crew
and himself from being holed with his crazy aero-
batics, the Catalina itself was punctured half a hundred times on the way to Henderson Field. Coming
in low to pull in to the field, Cram found he still had
one angry Zero on his tail. His airspeed was also too
high for a landing, so Cram continued on to the
satellite field, Fighter 1.

His luck improved over Fighter 1, for as he
waddled onto the strip one of the fighter pilots,
VMF-121's Lieutenant Roger Haberman, forced
out of the fighting with a smoking Wildcat, also
came in to the field. Seeing the Catalina under
attack, Haberman eased his Wildcat, its wheels already lowered for landing, onto the Zero pilot's
tail and shot the Zero out of the air.

When Geiger saw what remained of his command
plane he threatened Mad Jack Cram with a court-
martial for "deliberate destruction of government
property," and then awarded him the Navy Cross.

By the day's end the Japanese had lost three transports, which burned and had to be beached, with
much destruction to their cargoes. This included

*Major Jack R. Cram, aide and pilot for Marine Major
General Roy S. Geiger.*

supplies, artillery ammunition, and, of course,
troops. Even B-17s had come up from the New
Hebrides to sink one of the ships. Fighters, in addition to mixing with the Zeros, also strafed the
transports and the beaches, inflicting a terrible toll on
the Japanese troops. American losses were three
Dauntlesses and four Wildcats, but those Japanese
ships which had not been destroyed pulled away
from Tassafaronga.

Still, nearly five thousand troops had been landed
and the night was again rendered hideous by shelling from cruisers. On October 15 Geiger had only
thirty-four aircraft (nine Wildcats) to stand off any
Japanese attempt to retake Guadalcanal. The truth
was that all was not at all well in the Solomons.
While the word was not released to the American
public, the words of Admiral Nimitz were arresting:

Harold W. Bauer (in an early photograph), who earned a Medal of Honor on the day he arrived at Henderson Field, and was lost in combat before he could be decorated. (DEFENSE DEPT., MARINE CORPS)

"It now appears that we are unable to control the sea in the Guadalcanal area. Thus our supply of our positions will only be done at great expense to us. The situation is not hopeless, but it is certainly critical."

General Vandegrift was far less reticent when he informed Ghormley that it was "Urgently necessary that this force [i.e., Vandegrift's command on Guadalcanal] receive maximum support of air and surface units."

Ghormley was able to send additional Wildcats of VMF-212 (some of whose pilots were already at Henderson), under Lieutenant Colonel Harold W. Bauer. This put Geiger's fighter strength up to twenty-eight; also arriving with Bauer's flight were seven Dauntlesses which had accompanied them up from Efate (New Hebrides). As the formation set-

tled down for a landing late in the afternoon they found they had arrived in the middle of a dive-bombing attack. Nine Vals were working over the U.S.S. *McFarland,* which had just delivered a cargo of aviation fuel and was preparing to pull out of the Solomons with medical evacuees aboard.

Seeing this, and despite nearly empty fuel tanks after the long flight north, Bauer singlehandedly took after the Vals. He dived into the squadron of Japanese bombers and slashed through with his guns hammering; in minutes four Vals fell away burning. Bauer, now dangerously low on fuel, had to pull away and land at Henderson Field. He was to receive a Medal of Honor for this attack, but he did not survive to accept it.

v

The date of Bauer's Medal of Honor fight was October 16, 1942. On this same day Ghormley received word of great activity by the Japanese fleet in the vicinity of the Santa Cruz Islands, south and east of the Solomons. Ghormley recognized the situation as more than critical, wired Nimitz that his "forces [were] totally inadequate to meet" the impending threat. In two days, on October 18, 1942, Ghormley was out. He was replaced by a "more aggressive commander" (the words are Nimitz's) in the person of Vice-Admiral William F. Halsey. When word was released in the Pacific it was greeted by cheers from the men, who had been discouraged over the stalemate at Guadalcanal.

General Hyakutake, meanwhile, had formulated his plan of attack upon the Henderson perimeter; there would be three simultaneous assaults at widely separated points. The main push would come up from the south under Lieutenant General Masao Maruyama. A keen sense of history motivated the general, for he instructed his engineers to construct a trail through the swamp and jungle leading to Henderson Field, which he, free of false modesty, decided to name "the Maruyama Road." The total plan was elaborate, therefore complex, and like so many grand military enterprises, appeared fine on paper and sounded beautiful in high-level discussion, but proved to be much different when attempted "on the ground" and with live men instead of symbols.

Timed to coincide with Hyakutake's seizure of

Henderson Field, Yamamoto at Truk had impressive plans for the Combined Fleet. He assembled four carriers, five battleships, fourteen cruisers, and forty-four destroyers for an all-out effort which, it was planned, would settle the bothersome Solomons question once and for all. Yamamoto was emboldened by the knowledge that with the *Wasp* sunk and the *Saratoga* undergoing repairs, his only carrier opposition would come from the *Hornet*. He did not know, however, that the *Enterprise* had recovered from the three bomb hits taken in the Battle of the Eastern Solomons and was ready for action.

The land battle opened first, when Hyakutake's three-pronged attack got off to an unco-ordinated start on October 23. Communications being what they were in Guadalcanal's jungles, the neatly laid plans went quite readily awry. To soften up the American positions for Hyakutake's grand blow a large force of Japanese bombers with fighter escort came down from Rabaul and Buin. These were met by two dozen Marine and Navy Wildcats.

Climbing to meet the Japanese, Joseph Foss counted sixteen bombers and perhaps twenty-five Zeros. As he led his flight in an attack upon five Zeros, Foss found himself about to be victimized by twenty, which dived out of the sun. The Wildcats snapped into a fast dive to accumulate the speed to escape the enemy fighters. As he zoomed out of the way Foss caught a glimpse of a Wildcat on the tail of a Zero. Another Zero was attached to the Wildcat. Foss reacted immediately and the second Zero quickly, under his guns, disintegrated in mid-air. Foss, who witnessed several such explosions, described the process: "The motor goes off in a crazy, lopsided whirl. The pilot pops out of his cockpit like a pea that has been pressed from a pod. The air is filled with dust and little pieces, as if someone has emptied a huge vacuum cleaner bag in the sky. The wing section, burning where it had joined the fuselage, takes a long time to fall. It goes down like a leaf—sailing, then almost stopping as it attacks the air, sailing again, and attacking the air again." Foss was forced to turn sharply to avoid "the falling junk" as he whirled into another Zero. Before he was forced out of the fighting with a badly smoking engine, the result of a head-on attack by a Zero, which he also shot out of the sky, Foss had shot down four of the day's tally of twenty Zeros and four bombers.

Joseph J. Foss, USMC, who shot down twenty-six Japanese planes over the Solomons (twenty-three of them over Guadalcanal during the period October 9–November 19, 1942) to earn himself the Medal of Honor and the accolade of America's ace of aces until Richard Bong's score began accumulating over New Guinea. (DEFENSE DEPT., MARINE CORPS)

Rain on the next day discouraged all activity except for the Japanese troops slithering through the jungle over the prematurely named Maruyama Road. The day after, October 25, 1942, went down in Marine history as "Dugout Sunday." Thanks to the mud, most U.S. aircraft were immobilized when the Japanese planes came over in the morning and gave the Marine positions a severe mauling. Japanese land, sea, and air traffic picked up; the big final push was on.

American aircraft were unable to get off the airstrips until later in the day, but once they did they dealt severely with the Japanese. Once again Foss scored copiously, five Zeros in a single combat —bringing his total up to sixteen (his final score would be twenty-six). Dugout Sunday, which had begun so propitiously for the Japanese airmen, closed with a loss of twenty-two aircraft to fighters and four to antiaircraft guns.

Three hundred miles to the east of Guadalcanal, meanwhile, Yamamoto's Guadalcanal support force, the Third Fleet (Nagumo), and the Second Fleet (Kondo) waited. This powerful force was assigned the task of intercepting American attempts to reinforce the Guadalcanal garrison, presumably being torn to ribbons by Hyakutake's troops on the island, and also to prevent the survivors from escaping. Aware of the presence of the large Japanese naval forces to the north of the Santa Cruz Islands, Halsey ordered Task Force 61 (the *Enterprise*) and TF 17 (the *Hornet*), the only carrier forces available, to a rendezvous point north of the New Hebrides. To this was also added TF 64 (built around the battleship *Washington*). These forces were under the tactical command of Rear Admiral Thomas C. Kinkaid of the *Enterprise*.

The odds were far from even. Nagumo with his 4 carriers could count on 212 aircraft; Kinkaid had 171. There was but 1 American battleship to stand against 4 Japanese (as it eventuated, Task Force 64 did not participate in the battle, which left only the *South Dakota* of TF 61). To round out the picture: there were 12 Japanese cruisers versus 6 American, and 24 destroyers against 14. Nagumo exuded confidence for the first time since Midway, even more so, for he was not aware of the fact that the *Enterprise* had returned to active duty.

Still, Nagumo was uneasy. He awaited word of Vandegrift's surrender to Hyakutake, but it did not come. In fact, because of some confusion (and poor communications between the three broad arrows pointing toward Henderson Field on his field map), Hyakutake had been forced to postpone the concerted assault. Nagumo fretted and wired Hyakutake to get on with the American defeat, for the ships were running low on fuel. Then good word came from the island: Kawaguchi, of the ill-fated earlier fighting at Bloody Ridge, in an excess of hope was certain he saw some of his men overrun Henderson Field. A naval liaison officer with the ground troops sent the message, "Airfield taken." It was a premature conclusion, as it turned out, but it was enough for anxious Nagumo. He refueled and turned toward Guadalcanal, not knowing the Marines were blunting the land attack.

After midnight, October 25, 1942—Dugout Sunday on Guadalcanal—a Catalina out of Espiritu Santo found the Japanese fleet. The message sent was laconic: "Sighted enemy task force Lat. 'a' Long. 'b' course 'c' speed 'd' x-ray. Please notify next of kin." The Catalina, after dropping flares upon the Japanese force, shadowed the carriers for a time, attempting to collect more information. Then the big flying boat, low on fuel, turned away.

So did Nagumo, who reversed course. When Dauntlesses, Avengers, and Wildcats, launched from the *Enterprise* later in the day, fanned out searching for Japanese ships, Nagumo had slipped into the darkness and no enemy ships were found. The same frustration attended Nagumo. He was aware of the Americans and the increase of aerial and radio activity, but he had no real idea where their carriers were.

On October 26 all mystery was dispelled when a search plane from the *Shokaku* sighted the American forces bearing northwest. A search mission from the *Enterprise* also spotted Nagumo's carriers. There were no longer any military secrets as men began preparing for attacks upon the carriers in what came to be called the Battle of Santa Cruz.

Two Dauntlesses, one piloted by Lieutenant Stockton B. Strong and the other by Ensign Charles Irvine, came upon the big *Shokaku* and the small *Zuiho;* the *Zuikaku* was hidden under cloud some miles away. Strong signaled to Irvine that they would attack the nearest carrier, the *Zuiho,* so Irvine moved in closer, though behind Strong's Dauntless. So far so good, for they had moved into attack position without antiaircraft or Zero interference.

Strong rolled over, put his flaps in dive position, and with an eye on his aiming scope, plummeted toward the slender yellow deck of the *Zuiho*. Three hundred yards behind, Irvine followed. The Dauntlesses screamed down out of the sun until each reached a point about fifteen hundred feet above the *Zuiho,* which, Strong noted, carried no aircraft on its decks. Evidently a strike had already been launched by Nagumo. Strong released his five-hundred-pound bomb and seconds later Irvine's arched away from the belly of his Dauntless also. Both struck the *Zuiho* in the after section of the flight deck, ripping the deck open, toppling antiaircraft guns, and ending the *Zuiho* as an effective carrier for the rest of the battle. Although it would have been possible to launch aircraft, which he had already done, Captain Sueo Obayashi reported to Nagumo that the *Zuiho* would not be able to land any aircraft. The *Zuiho,* vulnerable and all but helpless, must leave the scene of combat.

Strong and Irvine, meanwhile, had pulled out of their dives, then sought the safety of near-water flight to escape the antiaircraft fire and the attacks by Zeros. While their rear gunners fought off the Zeros that came in too close, Strong radioed the location of the *Zuiho* and the amount of damage he estimated he and Irvine had done to it. Irvine's Dauntless had taken some hits in the wing and tail, which slowed him up a bit, as the two Navy planes strained at full speed for the *Enterprise.* The question was: Where would the *Enterprise* be? If it had come under observation, the ship would have certainly shifted course; if the Japanese planes, absent from the *Zuiho*'s flight deck, had found it, the situation could even be worse.

Finally, after a forty-five-mile chase, close to the waves and then dodging through puffs of cloud,

the Zeros gave up after losing two of their number to the Dauntless gunners. With practically no fuel the two Dauntlesses settled down upon the deck of the *Enterprise.* The time was ten twenty-six; the Dauntlesses had been air-borne since six that morning. They had done a good morning's work—and the *Enterprise,* thanks to a sudden local rain squall, had momentarily escaped attack.

At 5:15 A.M. Nagumo had launched the first attack group, under the command of Lieutenant Commander Mamoru Seki, from the *Shokaku* and the *Zuikaku.* For this strike the *Shokaku* had provided twenty-two Vals and twenty-seven Zeros; the *Zuikaku* put up eighteen Kates. Thus the strike was composed of dive bombers, torpedo bombers, and fighters. As the formation proceeded toward the American carriers they passed another group of aircraft going in the opposite direction. These were Dauntlesses from the *Hornet* on their way hoping to do hurt to the Japanese carriers. For some reason Lieutenant Commander Hideki Shingo, leading the *Shokaku*'s Zeros high above the bombers,

An Avenger of Air Group 10 prepares to take off from the Enterprise *at Santa Cruz. Hand-held signs give aircrews last-minute information; sign directly* *under the cowling reads: "Jap CV [carrier] Speed 25 at 8:30" and, directly over wheel, "Proceed without Hornet."* (NAVY DEPT., NATIONAL ARCHIVES)

A Kate passes over a cruiser, its target a carrier; Battle of Santa Cruz.

(NAVY DEPT., NATIONAL ARCHIVES)

did not see the *Hornet* formation, or did not recognize the planes as those of the enemy, so no attack was ordered. For this oversight Shingo's home ship would suffer. It was a ludicrous fraction of a moment as the bomber pilots, brothers under the skin though enemies, passed each other on similar errands. The good luck of the men of the *Hornet*'s first strike force would last until it found the Japanese ships.

Not so, however, for the men of the first *Enterprise* team. Eight Avengers, three Dauntlesses, and an escort of eight Wildcats took off early and headed for the presumed position of the Japanese carriers. Barely a half hour out from the *Enterprise* the formation suffered a sudden attack from above by Zeros. Almost simultaneously two Avengers, one of them flown by Lieutenant Commander John A. Collet, commander of Torpedo 10, spiraled burning into the ocean four thousand feet down. In the slashing attack by fighters from the already burning *Zuiho,* the *Enterprise* force was cut in half. The Wildcats, at a disadvantage at low altitude, were handicapped; three went down into the ocean and another, smoking, turned back for the *Enterprise,*

only about fifty miles away. When the survivors reassembled only four Avengers remained with the three Dauntlesses to make the attack and there were only four Wildcats to protect them.

But they did not find the carriers and dropped their bombs and torpedoes into what was believed to be "a *Kongo*-type" battleship. While the *Kongo* and the *Haruna* were units in Vice-Admiral Kondo's advance force, they were not hit that day. This was probably the *Chikuma,* a cruiser in Nagumo's striking force. Though struck and damaged rather heavily, the *Chikuma* continued to function despite casualties.

Though deprived of the Zero escort, which turned back after it had attacked the *Enterprise* force (because of fuel consumed in the fighting), Lieutenant Commander Seki led his Vals and Kates toward the *Hornet.* As combat air patrol Wildcats swept in to attack, Seki dived toward the *Hornet.* Heavy antiaircraft fire rose to hammer him and shortly after he had given his command for the attack, Seki was hit several times. His plane rolled over on its back, flame streaming behind, and continued toward the *Hornet.* Bombs were flung into the carrier

The Battle of Santa Cruz, October 26, 1942. The air filled with antiaircraft fire, the sea churning with the movement of heavy ships and plunging aircraft—and the Enterprise *(left) dodging a bomb or Japanese plane.*

from the Vals. A stricken Val, probably Seki's, came in upon the *Hornet,* careened off the stack, smashed through the flight deck, and burst with the detonation of its own bombs. And then the Kates came in, low on the water, to jab torpedoes into the carrier's sides. Two fish cut into the engineering spaces and the *Hornet,* spouting steam, flame, and gouts of black smoke, lurched to the starboard. During the torpedo attack another suicidal run was made on the *Hornet,* portent of things to come, when a Kate, which may have been that of Lieutenant Jiichiro Imajuku, ran in upon the *Hornet* from dead ahead (seemingly under control), smashed a gun gallery, rolled into a ball of flaming metal, and exploded near the forward elevator shaft.

The U.S.S. *Hornet,* Doolittle's "Shangri-La," was finished and truly could the Japanese at long last claim vengeance for the Tokyo raid. But for those who believe wars can be fought on vengeance, the *Hornet* would, before it sank into the Pacific, have its small share. Led by Lieutenant James E. Vose, the *Hornet*'s dive bombers located the *Shokaku* and broke through the screen of antiaircraft fire and Zeros. Bombs splashed across the deck of the *Shokaku,* Nagumo's flagship, splintering great holes in the deck and producing violent flames, twisting hot gun barrels out of action and starting fierce blazes below decks. Although the *Shokaku* was to escape the final fate of the *Hornet,* it was no longer capable of either taking or launching planes and its communications were out. Nagumo was forced to leave the battle. He turned over the command to Rear Admiral Kakuji Kakuda aboard the unharmed *Zuikaku* and fled northward for Truk. The *Shokaku* would be out of the war for nine months.

But the *Zuikaku* and the *Junyo* (the latter of

Kondo's advance force) were still very much in the battle. Vals and Kates from both these carriers found the *Enterprise*, and though the Japanese planes were badly mauled by fighters and heavy antiaircraft fire, three bombs struck the *Enterprise*, causing terrible fires and damage and resulting in the death of forty-four men. The Kates too added to the misery of the day, but skillful dodging under the cool command of Captain Osborne B. Hardison saved the *Enterprise* from further damage. Gunners of the *South Dakota,* a battleship armed with heavy AA batteries, destroyed Japanese planes attempting to hit the *Enterprise* also. The *South Dakota,* however, suffered a hit from one of the *Junyo* bombers. So did the cruiser *San Juan.* The destroyer *Smith* was crashed by a Kate, which set the ship aflame. And as it drew into the vicinity of the *Hornet* to take men from the burning carrier, the

To reduce the hazard of fire, a damaged Dauntless is pushed off the deck of the Enterprise *into the waters off Santa Cruz.* (NAVY DEPT., NATIONAL ARCHIVES)

destroyer *Porter* was torpedoed by Japanese submarine I-21. The *Porter* sank, taking fifteen men trapped in the firerooms, and later the *Hornet,* "a flaming mass," was sunk by the Japanese destroyers *Makikumo* and *Akigumo.*

The *Hornet* and *Porter* were the only ships, both American, which were lost in the Battle of Santa Cruz. Truly could the Imperial fleet make claims for a great victory in what they called "the Battle of the South Pacific." Despite the damages to the *Shokaku* and *Zuiho,* it could be said that Yamamoto had won the battle, but there was a subtle perplexity to consider. No Japanese ships had gone down, it was true, and the only carrier which sizzled under the sea was American, but under that sea also were sixty-nine Japanese aircraft totally lost, with an additional two dozen forced down into the sea. Some of the pilots from the latter were saved, but all the aircrews of the sixty-nine bombers and fighters, the few remaining veterans of Pearl Harbor, the Indian Ocean, and the Coral Sea, were lost.

Lieutenant Stanley W. "Swede" Vejtasa of VF-10, the Enterprise, *climbing into the cockpit of his Wildcat.* (NAVY DEPT., NATIONAL ARCHIVES)

If the Battle of Santa Cruz was frustrating in its lack of a clean-cut victory it was also obvious that American "carrier strength in the Pacific was now dangerously low," in the words of King. Even so, the Japanese had lost their last major attempt at taking back Guadalcanal. But the loss of so many experienced pilots, who might have trained more "sea eagles" for Nippon, was a heavy price to pay for the *Hornet* and the *Porter* and seventy-four U.S. planes.

Typical of the aerial action which marked the ferocity of the Santa Cruz battle was that engaged in by Lieutenant Stanley W. "Swede" Vejtasa. Leading three other members of VF-10 (the famed Lieutenant Commander James Flatley's "Grim Reapers" of the *Enterprise*) Vejtasa spent more than nine hours in the air on October 26, 1942. Shortly after Captain Hardison all but oscillated his

massive *Enterprise* out of the attack of five torpedo planes, Vejtasa and his four Wildcats were vectored to investigate more unidentified, incoming aircraft.

It had been an active flight, for Vejtasa had already destroyed two dive-bombing Vals, and upon reaching the new point, he saw no less than eleven Kates streaking for the *Enterprise*. If the Kates split up, as was customary, Hardison would have had to make the *Enterprise* dance to elude all of them. With his wingman, Lieutenant Leroy Harris, Vejtasa approached the stepped-up column of three Vs plus two Kates trailing. The other two men in his flight, Lieutenant Stanley E. Ruehlow and Ensign W. H. Leder, teamed up to attack. While Ruehlow and Leder were busy with a pair of Zeros, Vejtasa and Harris came in below and astern of the Kates. As soon as they were within range both men began firing and each took out one Kate, the two trailing the three V-formations. They pushed throttle to overtake the nine remaining Kates and just as they did entered a great cumulus cloud.

Vejtasa no longer saw Harris, but ahead of him, dimly, he could make out some Kates. He moved in, aimed at the left-hand member of the formation, and opened with his six .50-calibers. The Kate exploded and fell away. The next plane lost its rudder and then burst into flame and fell too. Alerted, the third Kate attempted to turn, but the faster Wildcat turned more sharply and Vejtasa opened up on the Japanese bomber. It had exposed its length to the spray of Vejtasa's guns and the last plane of the V splashed into the sea.

Low on ammunition, Vejtasa spotted another Kate, but it had pulled well away from him and he elected to leave it to the antiaircraft fire which awaited it. As he circled the arena of battling ships Vejtasa saw another Kate, obviously free of its torpedo, fleeing the scene. The Wildcat dived upon the bomber, and with his last few rounds Vejtasa knocked down his seventh enemy plane of the day. The four VF-10 Wildcats had so disrupted the Kate attack that three of the survivors jettisoned their torpedoes and fled. Two others did not even drop theirs, although the one Vejtasa had left for the ship's antiaircraft batteries may have been the Kate that crashed into the *Smith*.

The Battle of Santa Cruz ended, a tactical victory for the Japanese. The *Hornet* was gone and the *Enterprise* had been hit and crippled; this left only

". . . and the last plane . . . splashed into the sea."
The Battle of Santa Cruz, though it cost the Ameri- cans the Hornet *and crippled the* Enterprise, *cost the Japanese heavily in aircraft and experienced pilots.*
(NAVY DEPT., NATIONAL ARCHIVES)

two carriers in the Pacific, the *Enterprise* and the *Saratoga,* which was also crippled and undergoing repair. Wisely, Kinkaid pulled away to the south out of reach of Kondo's big ships and Kakuda's remaining aircraft. The *Zuikaku* and *Junyo* were still capable of dispatching bombers which might have spelled the end of the *Enterprise.* Nor could

Kinkaid risk the possibility of a night engagement for the simple reason that the Japanese were better at it at the time than the Americans. It was a frustrating engagement all around: the Japanese had won, but they had lost too many experienced pilots. The battle ashore, which the naval battle had been designed to cover, had failed.

4

DERAILING THE
TOKYO EXPRESS

GUADALCANAL remained in American hands. General Hyakutake's beautifully reasoned plan of attack and his formal, very proper surrender ceremony never came off. By October 28, with more than three thousand Japanese dead on Guadalcanal and sixty-nine irreplaceable pilots deep in the sea off Santa Cruz, it was obvious that another Japanese attempt to take the miserable island had miscarried. The island took on a significance beyond its strategic importance (which militarists eventually realized was secondary). The Allies were determined to keep it and the Japanese were resolved to take it back. It became for both sides as much a matter of "face" as military consequence.

But to the men garrisoned on "the Canal" it was much less a matter of face than skin. Keeping alive was the major preoccupation, of course—and scrounging simple comforts (like keeping dry). Even these basic pursuits became monotonous in day-after-day operations. But when the fighting came again, monotony was regarded with nostalgia. Between battles the Marines engaged in the art of bitching, their most colorfully profane antipathy being reserved for "Dugout Doug" MacArthur. The average line Marine was sure that only MacArthur's grabbing and holding of equipment, such as the P-38 for example, was responsible for the shoestring

operation on Guadalcanal. General Arnold of the Air Force was placed a few degrees above MacArthur, and almost on an equal level was General Marshall. At this time, actually, supplies that might have gone to the Pacific were being sent instead to Europe for the projected invasion of North Africa. But the so-called "Big Picture" was of little concern to the Marine who believed himself all but marooned on 'Canal.

Yamamoto, on Truk, was unhappy also. Despite all his attempts to co-ordinate the operations of the Imperial fleet with those of the Army, the Army had not yet taken back Guadalcanal. And this failure by the Army cost the Imperial Navy heavily in men, ships, and aircraft. The Army, on the other hand, could not understand that the Navy was unable to maintain its ships indefinitely at sea "consuming valuable fuel" while the Army fought out its inconclusive land battles.

As always, the solution must devolve upon the Imperial Navy. Obviously Hyakutake's error lay in attempting to take Henderson Field by land. Just as obviously—at least it appeared so to Yamamoto —Henderson must be taken from the sea by very heavy bombardment. This would ground the planes and keep the men in their foxholes while reinforcements were brought in. With Henderson pulverized, it would be no problem for Hyakutake's starving, ill-equipped, sick, and dying troops (plus reinforcements, of course, not so hungry and better equipped) to end the protracted, embarrassing wretchedness of Guadalcanal.

The plan, as outlined to Hyakutake by Captain Toshikazu Ohmae, Chief of Staff, Southeastern Fleet, seemed to make sense. While Tanaka's Tokyo Express brought reinforcements (the 38th Division) to Guadalcanal in eleven transports down The Slot (the channel between New Georgia and Santa Isabel islands northwest of Guadalcanal), a large force of battleships, a cruiser, and destroyers from Admiral Kondo's Second Fleet would subject Henderson Field and environs to a tremendous shelling. At the same time another force of Kondo's fleet would lay to the north of Savo Island to furnish distant cover. Close in, Vice-Admiral Gunichi Mikawa, with cruisers and destroyers, would provide close support for the landings of the 38th Division.

During the night of November 12/13, 1942, what has come to be known as the Battle of Guadalcanal erupted when the Japanese raiding force, under Vice-Admiral Hiroaki Abe, on its way to open the shelling upon Henderson, ran up against a handful of American ships under the command of Rear Admiral Daniel J. Callaghan. With his five cruisers and eight destroyers Callaghan took on Abe's two battleships (the *Hiei* and *Kirishima*), the cruiser *Nagara,* and fourteen destroyers.

For the next twenty-four deadly, confused minutes "one of the most furious sea battles ever fought," according to Admiral King, illuminated the dark night sky and rocked the air with savage gunfire. At close quarters the two fleets fought to a near standstill, with the heaviest loss on the American side. Four American destroyers and two cruisers were lost. The Japanese lost only two destroyers, but the battleship *Hiei* had been hit many times, which prevented the planned heavy bombardment of Henderson Field (for this failure Abe was relieved of his command). Callaghan paid the full price for this frustration, for he and nearly all of his staff aboard the *San Francisco* were killed when the bridge of the ship was struck. More than seven hundred American lives were lost in the nightmarish battle. But Abe had run and Henderson had been spared.

Also frustrated was "Tenacious" Tanaka, who

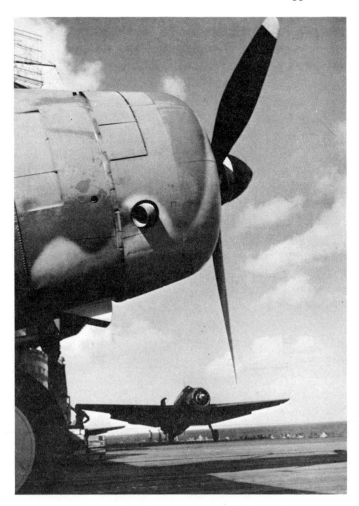

An Avenger on a takeoff run from the flight deck of the Enterprise. *Aircraft of this unit (CV-6) sank the first Japanese battleship of the war, the* Hiei *(with the aid of other Navy and Marine planes from Guadalcanal).* (NAVY DEPT., NATIONAL ARCHIVES)

was ordered to turn back from his Express run and await further word. While he fumed on his way back to the Shortland Islands, dawn came to Guadalcanal. Marine pilots in Dauntlesses and Avengers found the crippled *Hiei* just ten miles north of Savo Island. Though in trouble, the Japanese ship, screened by five destroyers, could still put up antiaircraft fire. But under the attack of the first ten planes, two torpedoes went into the side of the battleship. More Dauntlesses came shortly after and further harassed the stricken ship.

Meanwhile, as the damaged but operational *Enterprise* plowed northward for Guadalcanal, nine Avengers escorted by six Wildcats were dispatched

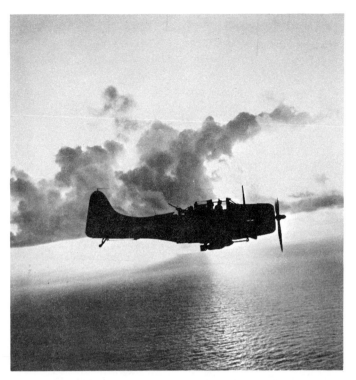

Dauntless on morning patrol in the Pacific.
(NAVY DEPT., NATIONAL ARCHIVES)

less destructive than previously, partly because they had been harassed during their bombardment by little PT boats from Tulagi, which had flitted distractingly around them.

On November 14, 1942, Tanaka, all but certain that Henderson Field had really been put out of commission by the night naval bombardments, raced his Express down The Slot with the largest number of reinforcements to date (three thousand men of a combined naval landing force and eleven thousand troops of Lieutenant General Tadayoshi Sano's 38th Division). The eleven transports were screened by a dozen destroyers and a small umbrella of Zeros from the light carrier *Hiyo.*

At 9:49 A.M. Lieutenant Doan Carmody, flying a search Dauntless from the *Enterprise,* now closer to Guadalcanal, found the transports in The Slot. The ships were 120 miles from Guadalcanal, making fourteen knots; the Express was due to arrive at the island around seven in the evening. After radioing this information to the *Enterprise,* Carmody, in company with another Dauntless (pilot: Lieutenant W. E. Johnson), dived upon the Japanese ship formation in The Slot. Both missed with their bombs, however, because of heavy antiaircraft fire and the quick action of seven Zeros of Tanaka's air cover. Johnson's SBD fell into the sea and two Zeros swooped down to spray the splash point and the debris. During the next few hours, this depredation would be heavily avenged.

If ever there was a hell on earth, it was carried on Tanaka's eleven transports that November 14. With merciless desperation, fed by the knowledge that more Japanese reinforcements on Guadalcanal could be fatal, Marine and Navy aircraft assaulted the Tokyo Express. All afternoon every flyable plane on Guadalcanal, plus others from the *Enterprise,* fully loaded with bombs or torpedoes, raced to The Slot. Despite the whirring Zeros, of which there were only a few thanks to the hesitant Kondo 150 miles to the north, who sent small numbers from time to time from his two carriers, the Dauntlesses and Avengers ripped into the Japanese ships. Thousand-pound bombs rained onto the decks of the transports and torpedoes slashed into their sides. Even the Wildcats, when they ran out of Zeros, dived to water level to strafe the crowded decks.

The first attack, made by eighteen Marine Dauntlesses led by Major Joseph Sailer, Jr. (VMSB-132)

to the island. As they came into Guadalcanal the *Enterprise* pilots spotted the *Hiei.* While the Wildcats discouraged the lurking Zeros the Avengers, led by Lieutenant Albert P. Coffin, swooped down upon the Japanese battleship and put three more torpedoes into it. This continued for most of the day as Marine and Navy aircraft ran a bomb shuttle between the *Hiei* and Guadalcanal. In the fighting eight Zeros were destroyed. They too had failed in this mission, for by night the ship, abandoned and scuttled by its crew, sank into the Pacific —the first Japanese battleship to be sunk by American forces.

Despite this upset, Yamamoto's plan proceeded. The following night (November 13/14) was torn by a thousand eight-inch shells lobbed into Henderson from cruisers sent from Rabaul. No great damage was done, though two Wildcats were completely destroyed and fifteen others pocked by shell fragments. These, along with a holed Dauntless, were repaired and ready to fly by the next day. None of the eight P-38s sent down by MacArthur only the day before suffered any damage, however. The holes in Fighter 1 were quickly filled. The Japanese ships had proved

A beached, burned-out Japanese troop transport the morning after the "Buzzard Patrol," which literally slaughtered the men and ships of the Tokyo Express November 13–14, 1942.

(DEFENSE DEPT., MARINE CORPS)

and Major Robert Richard (VMSB-142), plus seven Avengers led by Lieutenant Albert P. Coffin of the *Enterprise*'s VT-10, scored hits on three transports and a cruiser. More *Enterprise* pilots, under Lieutenant Commander James R. Lee, joined in what became by midday virtual slaughter.

But true to his nickname, Tanaka tenaciously pressed on, leaving a transport here and there en route in his bloody wake. Transports lay dead in the water burning, some split open spilling men, dead and injured into the churning water, as destroyers circled in an attempt to rescue men as well as fight off the attacking American planes. The carnage on the Japanese transports, inhumanly overcrowded to begin with, was ineffably obscene. For the packed though human cargo of the transports the hours, for those who had hours, between about twelve-thirty and nightfall were one shattering crescendo of terror, pain, and death. And there was no place to hide.

Some American fighter pilots, who had come in close enough to see the butchery on the transports as well as the encrimsoned waters around them, were literally sickened by the sight. Some vomited in their cockpits. But they machine-gunned the thousands of bobbing heads in the water, the helpless near-drowned clinging to debris and wreckage. By 4:45 P.M., when the final strike took off from Henderson—led by Glen Estes of the *Enterprise*'s VS-10: four Dauntlesses (three of which were Marine) and fighter cover—seven Japanese transports had been sunk or were sinking or burning or both. Estes dropped the last bomb of the day, made a direct hit and returned to Henderson.

The four surviving transports were in bad shape also, but Tanaka proceeded to Guadalcanal. Sometime after midnight he arrived, quite depleted, at his destination. There was nothing to do but beach the crippled transports. About 3000 troops were landed with a mere 260 cases of ammunition and 1500 bags of rice. The rest of their supplies and perhaps another 3000 of their comrades lay at the bottom of The Slot, dead or missing. Of those who had escaped the slaughter of what the Americans came to call the "Buzzard Patrol," less than 2000 were picked up out of the water. Exact figures may

The forward deck of one of the beached Japanese transports after attacks by American planes and ships.
(DEFENSE DEPT., NATIONAL ARCHIVES)

Henderson to organize a rescue party. Despite an intensive search Bauer was never found.

II

The closing phase of the Battle of Guadalcanal, which had opened so disastrously for the Americans but which developed into a Japanese tragedy, was another nighttime surface battleship brawl. Vice-Admiral Kondo approached Guadalcanal to shell the airfield to cover the landings of Tanaka's "sorry remnant" (Tanaka's phrase) with the battleship *Kirishima* (sister ship of the *Hiei,* lost the day before), five cruisers, and nine destroyers.

Kondo ran into an American naval group (battleships *Washington* and *South Dakota* and four destroyers), under the capable command of Rear Admiral Willis Augustus Lee, in the vicinity of Iron Bottom Bay. Though in the battle which opened before midnight of November 14 Lee had lost three destroyers and the *South Dakota* was damaged, Kondo lost one destroyer and, most importantly, the *Kirishima* (so badly damaged that it was scuttled). The great battleship sank in waters close to the *Hiei,* and with it went Kondo's brilliant career. He had failed once again to ravage Henderson Field.

The common soldier behind Japanese lines by late December was certain that he had been abandoned. "Have not seen one of our planes in ages," one confided to his diary, "but every day enemy planes dance in the sky. . . ." It was a dance of death, for the strafing, dive-bombing, and bombing cut off supplies, reinforcements, and medical necessities.

While great men, irresolute yet unyielding, grappling with ego rather than conscience, sought a face-saving solution, little men died in mass, faceless numbers. At last, after weeks of acrid argument, two men called at the Imperial Palace on the final day of 1942. They were an admiral, Osami Nagano, Chief of the Naval Staff, and a general, Hajime Sugiyama, the Army's Chief of Staff. They had arrived unsmiling and they left unsmiling, but when they did leave it was with grim permission from Hirohito himself. The Japanese would abandon Guadalcanal.

Sometime during the first week of February 1943 the Tokyo Express was scheduled to run in reverse. This odious operation was a carefully guarded

never be determined, but Tanaka's determination—and the determination of the Buzzard Patrol—had wiped out about half of the largest attempt by the Tokyo Express. Every transport was lost, for the four beached ships were worked over the following day by aircraft, the destroyer *Meade,* and artillery.

The cost to the Americans was comparatively light: six Dauntlesses and two Wildcats. One of the latter was that of Lieutenant Colonel Joseph Bauer (VMF-212), who had gone out to escort the bombers. In company with Joseph Foss, Bauer had strafed a transport, after which both pilots were attacked by Zeros. Bauer shot one out of the air and Foss took off after the other. Antiaircraft fire from a Japanese destroyer spoiled the chase for Foss, who returned to the spot where he had last seen Bauer. Circling low over the water, Foss found pieces of the fallen Zero. About two miles away, swimming near an oil slick, Foss spotted Bauer in the water.

Circling, Foss attempted to eject his rubber boat, but found he was unable to because it was jammed. He circled again, lower, and realized that Bauer, bouncing and gesticulating in the water, was ordering him to return to base. Foss also found he could not radio for assistance, so he throttled back to secret; even officers (except of exalted rank) on Guadalcanal had no idea of what was happening. New troops were even brought in to conceal the true plan. All of the activity appeared to the watchful Americans like the beginnings of a real push on Guadalcanal. "Until the last moment it appeared that the Japanese were attempting a major reinforcement effort," Admiral Nimitz wrote in retrospect. "Only skill in keeping their plans disguised and bold celerity in carrying them out enabled the Japanese to withdraw the remnants of the Guadalcanal garrison."

By February 8, 1943, after six months of appalling fighting, Guadalcanal was taken over by the Americans. Like Midway, it marked a turn in the tide from the defensive to the offensive and it was the first defeat on land experienced by the victory-drunk Japanese Army. At the same time, although he fought ferociously and often as not to an existential, sacrificial death, the Japanese soldier had proved not to be a jungle superman. The myth was over for the Japanese soldier just as it was for the Zero, the super fighter plane.

Jefferson J. DeBlanc, one of the "few Marines," with Medal of Honor awarded for leading his flight into a large Japanese fighter formation before it could interfere with American Dauntlesses and Avengers.
(DEFENSE DEPT., MARINE CORPS)

III

Although the Japanese were out of Guadalcanal, it did not mean that the Solomons were entirely abandoned by them. Late in November 1942 preparations for constructing an airfield on Munda Point, New Georgia, were noted by Allied reconnaissance planes; so was construction on some of the smaller islands of the New Georgia group, Kolombangara and Vella Lavella. An airfield on Munda Point, however, meant only a 175-mile flight to Henderson Field, which placed it within easy reach of the Zero. And at the top of the Solomons there was Bougainville, with no less than five airfields, the largest of which was Kahili, near the southern tip of the island. If the Americans had paid heavily for Henderson Field, the Japanese had full intentions of exacting a high and bloody interest on it.

Attempts were made to discourage the building up of the new Japanese positions, now the new terminals for the Tokyo Express. Between the hard days of October, when the Americans might have been pushed out of Guadalcanal, and the nearly

magical spiriting away of the Japanese in February, there were times when the fighting became as intense as in the shoestring days. On one mission, January 31, 1943, a young Marine lieutenant, Jefferson Joseph DeBlanc, a section leader in VMF-112, was assigned to escort Dauntlesses and Avengers to bomb enemy shipping in Vella Gulf. The target area lay less than fifty miles east and slightly north of the Japanese air base on Kolombangara Island.

Upon arriving at Vella Gulf the Marine formation was met by a large number of enemy fighters. DeBlanc led his six Wildcats into the mass of Zeros at fourteen thousand feet, hoping to keep them away from the bombers while they worked over the shipping. As the battle developed, it broke up into single Wildcats against several Zeros. DeBlanc dived down to the altitude at which the dive bombers were trying to operate only to find he had swept into a large formation of float planes (probably the Mitsubishi A6M2-N, an adaptation of the Zero and called the "Rufe" by the Allies). Slashing into the Rufes, DeBlanc quickly sent three of them down burning, thus breaking up their concentration on the Dauntlesses, which proceeded to harass the Japanese surface ships in the gulf.

In the fighting DeBlanc's Wildcat had been hit and he was low on fuel. He realized he would have to return to Guadalcanal, so he climbed to get his bearings and as much height as he could. As he nursed the Wildcat up to the high clouds, DeBlanc, twisting his neck in the traditional fighter pilot fashion, spotted two Zeros closing from behind. He was now alone, for the other Wildcats were spread across the sky in their own private battles and the Dauntlesses and Avengers were engaged in bombing the Japanese ships.

DeBlanc would have to fight it out, though a stricken Wildcat was a poor match for a Zero. Timing his rudder kick for the precise moment, DeBlanc jerked the Wildcat into the path of the attacking Zeros. A good hit sent one rocketing across the sky as the other flashed by, turned, and came back at the Wildcat. DeBlanc felt the Grumman shuddering under the strain of his maneuvers and the impact of enemy slugs. As the Zero raced in, its guns twinkling maliciously, DeBlanc turned sharply again and shattered the frail Japanese plane with all four of his guns. The Zero fluttered down to the sea.

Safe now, DeBlanc found himself in other peril. The Wildcat was now in such poor condition that he knew he would never make it back to Guadalcanal. Smoking and with engine heaving badly, the plane started down for the water. DeBlanc fought with the plane to keep it from plowing into the ocean as he straightened out practically at treetop height over Kolombangara. Clearing the Japanese-held island, DeBlanc steadied the Wildcat out to sea and at a dangerously low altitude took to his chute. Upon landing in the water he found that he had been wounded in the back, arms, and legs. Supported by his lifejacket, DeBlanc spent about six hours making his way back to the beach at Kolombangara. Luckily he was not found by the Japanese but, after subsisting for two days on coconuts, was found instead by friendly islanders, who turned him over to the local coastwatcher. In about two weeks a Catalina arrived off Kolombangara to pick up DeBlanc as well as Staff Sergeant James A. Feliton, who had parachuted during the same battle as had DeBlanc. The latter was immediately sent to a hospital to recuperate and was awarded the Medal of Honor.

On the same day that Lieutenant DeBlanc and Sergeant Feliton were taken off Kolombangara and only six days after the last living Japanese soldier had been evacuated from Guadalcanal, a curious incident occurred over Bougainville.

Navy PB4Ys (the Army's B-24, Liberator) had taken off to bomb targets on Bougainville—no mean round trip of six hundred miles—with an escort of new fighters.

As the American bombers and fighters approached Bougainville, a lone Zero pilot ignored the war momentarily in order to fly alongside the new fighters to study them with peacetime inquisitiveness. Before he was driven off the Japanese pilot saw a strange-looking plane, half beautiful and half ugly. It was deep blue in color with a pale blue, almost white underside. The pilot sat way back on the fuselage under a bubblelike canopy; a great stretch of nose projected before him, ending in a wide cowling under which roared a massive eighteen-cylinder Pratt and Whitney "Twin Wasp" engine. Its most curious feature was the graceful inverted gull wing which jutted down and then up and away from the fuselage. Once seen, this aircraft was not mistaken for any other: it was the Chance Vought F4U-1, the "Corsair." American ground troops called it "the Bent Winged Bird" in time.

The Corsair, which had arrived at Henderson Field on February 12 flown by VMF-124, had originally been designed as a carrier fighter. Problems developed during carrier landing tests, because of the plane's long nose, which interfered with the pilot's vision. It also had a tendency to bounce upon touching the deck and had other bugs, which discouraged the Navy from stationing the plane on carriers for a time. Meanwhile, it was turned over to the Marines, in whose hands, and later also the Navy's, the Corsair proved to be one of the outstanding fighters of the war. Some Japanese pilots, in fact, regarded it as the most formidable American fighter of the war. It was faster than any Japanese plane, besides which it could climb much faster (about three thousand feet a minute) and had a greater range capability than any single-engined

Newly arrived Corsairs at Guadalcanal being prepared for combat. The plane in the foreground is having its *guns bore-sighted with a homemade device.*
(C. L. SMITH/DEFENSE DEPT., MARINE CORPS)

fighter operating in the Pacific at the time. And it was rugged, which suited the hardened Marines perfectly.

But it would take time to learn how to use the Corsair's capabilities fully. This was demonstrated on the day following the incident with the curious Zero pilot in what became known as "the Saint Valentine's Day Massacre." Navy Liberators, on a bombing mission to Kahili airfield, Bougainville, were escorted by P-40s (low cover), P-38s (high cover), and Corsairs of VMF-124, staggered in between. This became the standard pattern for missions at this time, with the bombers at around twenty thousand feet and the P-38s and Corsairs above them. On this day, however, the system did not function too well, for as the formation approached

Kahili it was bounced by perhaps fifty Zeros (almost certainly alerted and waiting). Two Liberators went down, as did two P-40s, two Corsairs, and, worse, the entire top cover of four P-38s. Japanese losses came to three or four Zeros, one as result of a collision with a Corsair.

This action, generally used to reveal how the Corsair nearly failed in its first test of real combat, is actually a better exemplification of the not yet (or ever, for that matter) dampened zeal of the Japanese fighter pilot. And, too, the "Zeke," as the Zero by this time was coming to be called, was still a formidable plane in a melee. But in the Corsair the Zeke had met its nemesis; it would only take a little time, a little experience, and a few Marines to establish this.

Allied fighter pilot's view of a "Zeke," on the tail.
(U. S. AIR FORCE)

But the problem of the inexperienced pilot was becoming even more serious for the Japanese, whose first-line veterans had been lost at Midway and Guadalcanal and whose new pilots were poorly trained for lack of experienced pilots to teach them. The American situation was differently handled, for when it was possible (and if they survived) veteran pilots were taken out of combat and given assignments training young fighter pilots. This is what happened with John Smith, Marion Carl, and Joseph Foss after they had left Guadalcanal. When Smith attempted to return to combat duty he was emphatically told, "Not until you have trained a hundred and fifty John Smiths." When he did return, almost two years later, Smith flew a Corsair.

IV

The Marines and their Corsairs owned the air over the Solomons and Kenney's Kids had begun "to play in the back yard of the Nip" in New Guinea; it was an ignominious situation to stomach in Tokyo. With the loss of Guadalcanal and then,

within a month, the Battle of the Bismarck Sea, Imperial headquarters burned with a hard, brittle flame of revenge. Yamamoto himself took full command of this vengeance operation, called *I-go Sakusen* ("Operation A"), a newly devised plan directly generated by the turn of fortune in the Pacific. *I-go Sakusen* was to wipe out, once and for all, the total American air power from the Solomons and New Guinea.

Planning *I-go Sakusen* for early April 1943, Yamamoto established his headquarters at Rabaul, major target of Kenney's forces in New Guinea and the major goal of Halsey's forces, climbing up the bloody Solomons ladder. Loath to expose his few remaining carriers to American aircraft, Yamamoto nonetheless stripped all carrier planes from their respective ships. Those from the 1st Carrier Division (the *Zuikaku* and *Zuiho*) went to Rabaul under command of Vice-Admiral Jisaburo Ozawa (who since November 16, 1942, had replaced Nagumo as commander of the Third Fleet). The aircraft of the 2nd Carrier Division (the *Junyo* and *Hiyo*) were flown to the base at Ballale, just south of Bougainville. The 21st Koku Sentai was to operate from Kavieng at the northern tip of New Ireland under Rear Admiral Toshinosuka Ichimaru (although the main body was stationed at Rabaul under command of Ozawa). The 26th Koku Sentai (Rear Admiral Kanae Kozaka) would strike from Kahili. In all, Yamamoto amassed about 350 warplanes for his strikes, Zekes, Nells, Bettys, Kates, and a few Vals. He was decidedly out for blood.

The first large assault came shortly after noon on April 7, 1943, when coast watchers and radar operators reported massive formations of enemy aircraft heading for Guadalcanal. There were, in fact, no less than 67 Vals escorted by 110 Zekes. The warning went out to ships in the harbor and to the men at Henderson, "Condition *very* Red."

The attack was met by all possible flyable fighters, seventy-six, Army, Navy, and Marine: P-38s, P-39s, Corsairs, and Wildcats. In the heavy fighting which followed, some of the Vals broke through the American fighter defenses and sank several ships in Tulagi Harbor and off Guadalcanal (the tanker *Kanawha,* the destroyer *Aaron Ward,* and the Australian corvette *Moa*).

First Lieutenant James E. Swett, of Marine VMF-221, on his first combat mission, ran into some of

James E. Swett, USMC, who broke up a Japanese dive bomber attack (for which he received the Medal of Honor) and became an ace on his first combat mission. (DEFENSE DEPT., MARINE CORPS)

the Japanese attackers. Leading a division of four Wildcats toward Tulagi, Swett spotted a large formation of Vals within minutes of arriving. There were between fifteen and twenty Japanese planes headed for Tulagi Harbor; shouting "Tally Ho!" Swett dived into the Vals. But even before he could begin shooting—for the first time in combat—he heard more shouting in his earphones. Someone else in his division had spotted Zekes diving from above. Already in a steep dive aimed at the dive bombers, Swett concentrated on the immediate menace and, as his Medal of Honor citation was to read, "during his dive personally exploded three hostile planes in mid-air with accurate and deadly fire."

Separated from the rest of his division, Swett was forced to do the best he could, what with the heavy concentration of "friendly" antiaircraft fire bursting around him—and six additional Vals, which bore onward toward the ships. One of his guns, too, was inoperative, so he had but five 50s with which to contend with the enemy formations. Racing in behind the Vals, Swett soon learned that the five guns worked well on the Vals, and the fourth plane swept away burning and trailing bits and pieces.

And so it went on until he shot down two more Vals, making his total for the battle seven—he had become an ace in his first combat. But as he closed in on the last of his victims Swett's Wildcat was hit by the fire of the Val's rear gunner. As his canopy shattered, blood covered his face, but Swett continued firing until his guns no longer responded: he had exhausted his ammunition. But before he did, he saw that the gunner in the rear cockpit of the Val had slumped over and smoke had begun to wisp out of the Val.

Swett's own problems were too many for him to worry about making certain that his eighth victim crashed into the waters of Iron Bottom Bay (his official score stood then at seven). He himself was injured by the flying bits of the canopy, and with his engine temperature in the red, Swett realized that the Japanese gunner had hit his Wildcat's lubricating system. The Pratt and Whitney growled and thumped, grew hot, and finally fused, and the propeller froze.

Too low now to take to his chute, Swett prepared to ditch off Florida Island. As he brought the Wildcat down near the water he suffered further consideration from "friendly" AA. Then the Wildcat splashed into Iron Bottom Bay, bounced and smacked into the water again. Swett, though held in his seat by straps, was thrown forward, smashing his nose against the gun sight. It took some time, after this stunning impact, for the pilot to place all things into focus. He knew he must get out of the swiftly sinking Wildcat. But he could not, for with a muddled, pain-racked head, he was not thinking clearly. As the plane sank Swett found that his chute harness had caught on a small handle in the cockpit.

As the Wildcat swirled down to the bottom, Swett continued to struggle until the strap loosened from the handle, which at the same time ejected the life raft stored in the plane. Suffocating, Swett finally surfaced with the help of a hastily inflated "Mae West," although encumbered by parachute, flying clothes, and the uninflated life raft. More struggling freed him and he inflated the raft and crawled, hurting and bleeding, into it. In a short time he was picked up by a small boat, whose passengers carried rifles as a precaution. Japanese pilots had demonstrated a deadly aversion to rescue, often attempting to kill their would-be Samaritans.

Yamamoto's revenge operation I-go Sakusen *was a simultaneous series of fruitless (but not always completely) strikes upon Guadalcanal and New Guinea. On April 12, 1943, more than a hundred Japanese aircraft struck the Fifth Air Force base at Port Moresby,* *New Guinea, setting an oil dump aflame with heavy loss of fuel and lubricants. Yamamoto's "Operation A" was his final contribution to Japan's war effort before he was shot down. He died believing the operation had been successful, which, in fact, it had not been.* (U. S. AIR FORCE)

"Are you an American?" someone shouted from the boat to Swett in his dinghy.

"You're damn right I am," he answered.

"It's OK," the voice was heard to say, according to legend; "he's another one of those loud-mouthed Marines."

Yamamoto's first big blow of *I-go Sakusen* had proved rather expensive, for claims were put in that day for a hundred planes by pilots and AA gunners. The actual number was closer to thirty-nine (twelve Vals and twenty-seven Zekes; Japanese postwar figures admit to the loss of twelve Vals but only nine Zekes). American losses for the day amounted to seven aircraft but only one pilot, Major Walden Williams of the 70th Fighter Squadron.

Yamamoto's other big raids were aimed at New Guinea, and he believed that by April 14, according to the claims of his pilots, Operation A had fulfilled its function. Four days later Yamamoto crashed in a burning Betty after being intercepted

Kenneth Walsh, USMC, first to achieve acedom in a Corsair. (DEFENSE DEPT., MARINE CORPS)

by P-38s over Kahili. Yamamoto's successor, Admiral Mineichi Koga, although not as brilliant a man, continued to practice the great man's philosophy—perhaps with less intensity—and did all he could to bloody the rungs of the Solomons ladder.

By the close of April more Corsairs had come into Guadalcanal, and by May 13, 1943, the first Corsair ace was brought to the fore. He was Lieutenant Kenneth Walsh of VMF-124, born in Brooklyn and who began his military career as a flying private in the Marines. During one of the preliminary phases of Yamamoto's Operation A, on April 1, 1943, Walsh shot down his first three Zekes. On the day of Yamamoto's big blow, Walsh, like Swett, was shot down but was pulled out of the water unhurt and was soon back flying a new Corsair. On May 13 in mixed company of Marine and Army fighters, Walsh encountered twenty-five Zekes escorting a Japanese photo plane. Admiral Koga was bringing more and more planes into Rabaul and he was most anxious to know all about the aviation facilities on Guadalcanal. There were, in fact, four airfields by this time.

During the battle with the Japanese formation, Walsh shot down three Zekes; he was officially an ace. The Japanese lost sixteen fighters, although the

photo plane escaped. Three Corsairs were lost in the fighting, one of them flown by Walsh's squadron commander, Major William Gise.

Meanwhile, American troops began taking and occupying other islands in the Solomons, each step bringing them closer to Bougainville, gateway to Rabaul. The Russell Islands were occupied in February; next in line came Munda (New Georgia), the battle for which opened on June 21. Soon it was possible for the Marines to operate from a forward base on Munda for the strike on Vella Lavella, next step up the ladder. In doing this, Halsey elected to bypass Kolombangara (garrisoned by ten thousand Japanese troops), which would place American planes within ninety miles of Kahili on Bougainville.

The Vella Lavella landings took place on August 15; although the action on the beaches was reasonably normal, Japanese aerial activity was furious. Bombers and fighters came down from Kahili, Ballale, and Buin (in spite of American bombings aimed at grounding the Japanese planes during the landings) to harass the ships and troops on the beachhead. That day Kenneth Walsh was leading a division of five Corsairs of VMF-124; his score by this time had risen to ten enemy aircraft.

Fresh from a recreation tour in Sydney, Australia, Walsh was unexpectedly surprised by five Zekes at ten thousand feet. The fight became generally confused and Walsh soon found himself alone chasing a Zeke away from the battle. The powerful Corsair caught up with the Japanese fighter after a five-mile chase and with one quick blast Walsh knocked the plane down. Turning back for the beachhead, Walsh inadvertently flew into a formation of nine Vals, on their way to bomb the beach. Coming from under the Vals, Walsh quickly lessened their number by two. But he was now in a tough spot: Vals, with their rear gunners, below him and Zekes above. His Corsair became the center of destructive attention. Diving Zekes put two large 20-mm. holes through his right wing, more peppering knocked out his hydraulic system, shreds of his horizontal stabilizer flew off into the slipstream, and, still unknown to Walsh, the right tire was holed.

With his superior speed capability, Walsh rapidly pulled away from the shooting gallery. Other pilots took over the fighting (in addition to the three Japanese planes shot down by Walsh, fourteen others

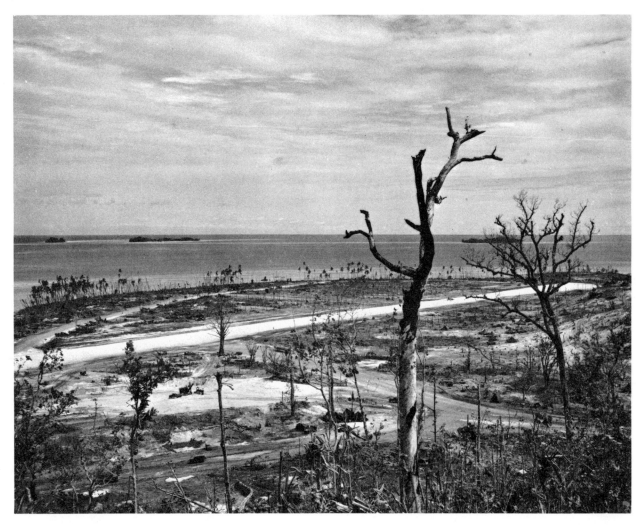

Munda Point airfield, New Georgia. Trees show effects of bombing and artillery fire—American and Japanese.
(DEFENSE DEPT., MARINE CORPS)

fell in the day's fighting) as Walsh guided his tattered Corsair home. He brought it in to Munda Field (which was just one day old) and as anxious Marines observed, landed the Corsair with hardly a bump, even compensating for the flat right tire. When Walsh stood in the cockpit he was cheered by the troops for bringing in so badly mauled an aircraft. The plane, in fact, was junked.

Fifteen days later Walsh returned to Guadalcanal and took part in a bombing mission to Kahili. The plan was to take off from Fighter 2, fly to the Russell Islands air base, take on plenty of fuel for the expected battle over Kahili, and join up with the Liberators. Then the two dozen bombers with two squadrons of Corsairs as well as the usual low-cover P-39s and P-40s would press on to Bougainville. All went well for Walsh until after he had taken off from the Russells. To his dismay his engine lost power and he could not keep up with the formation. Signaling to his wingman, Lieutenant W. P. Spencer, that he would have to drop out, Walsh, instead of attempting to return to the Russells or Fighter 2, guided his Corsair toward New Georgia with its advance base at Munda. Pushing his Corsair into a dive, Walsh brought the wheezing Corsair down onto the strip at Munda. There he was met by Captain James Neefus, commanding VMF-221, to whom he explained his problem and asked for another plane. Without recourse to red tape, Neefus permitted Walsh to requisition a ready, fueled, and armed Corsair on stand-by. Walsh jumped out of his plane and into the other; within

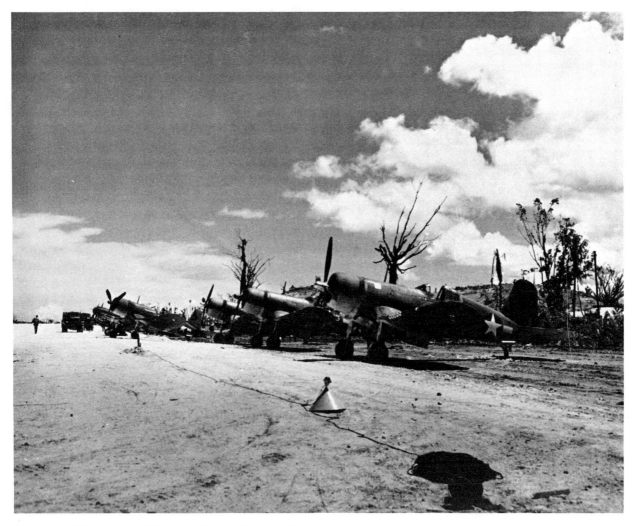

Corsairs on Munda—the Marine fighters arrived within a week after the airstrip was taken from the Japanese.
(CHESTER L. SMITH/DEFENSE DEPT., MARINE CORPS)

minutes he raced down the runway and after the large Kahili-bound formation.

Walsh pushed the throttle in order to rejoin the bombers and at the same time he pulled the Corsair up as high as it could go—about thirty thousand feet before he spotted aircraft ahead. Happy that he had caught up, he gunned his engine and found he had caught up, instead, with a formation of from forty to fifty Zekes. Soon after, he also saw the Liberators, some distance beyond the large formation of enemy fighters, under attack by Zekes and antiaircraft. A great air battle developed over Kahili as fighters from Kahili, Ballale, and Buin took to the air. Walsh, still undetected by the Japanese intent upon the bombers, pulled in behind the Zekes. He

was able to knock down only two before the others realized that a lone Corsair was pecking away at their formation.

The battle became a confused melee as Zekes turned on Walsh, who dived through the Liberator formation, shouting warnings on his radio. With the large number of planes in the air it became difficult to sight on any one of them and be certain he was an enemy. The sky became crisscrossed with tracers and, from time to time, a burning Liberator falling, for the Zekes were especially aggressive. The bombing run completed, the bombers turned away for the flight back to Henderson. During this phase of the battle Walsh destroyed two more Zekes, but he had had just about all the luck possible for the day. As he followed his fourth victim down to observe its fiery splash, Walsh, in turn,

was trailed by four Zekes. They boxed him in, and
with the advantage of altitude (and the fact that
Walsh had just about expended his ammunition),
they began working him over with cannon and machine-gun fire.

Smoke streamed from under the Corsair's cowling,
fuel pressure dropped, the engine churned. The
only other sound was that of Japanese lead pounding away at the tough Corsair. Walsh was about
ready to resign to fate when a P-40 and a few Corsairs came in to take the Zekes off his back. But,
though spared the final blow, Walsh knew he could
not make it to any base. He must ditch off Vella
Lavella. With consummate grace Walsh bounced
the gull-winged craft into the Pacific a mile off
Barakoma Point, where American Seabees, working
on a new airstrip, observed the smoking plane.

The great plane splashed in, leaving a foamy
wake, bumped up, and splashed again, then stopped
and began to settle. Walsh had hardly been shaken
and quickly left the Corsair and dropped into the
water. Within half an hour a Seabee boat came
out to pick him up and by the next day Walsh was
returned to Guadalcanal. When he was ordered back
to the United States in November 1943 Walsh, a
Medal of Honor recipient, had destroyed twenty
enemy aircraft (his twenty-first was scored during
his second tour of duty in 1945).

With Vella Lavella in American hands and Kolombangara all but ignored (the Japanese evacuated
the island in September–October), the next prize was
to be Bougainville. This was the largest and northernmost island of the Solomons—with Rabaul but 210
miles away. With the experience of Guadalcanal behind them it was decided by the South Pacific planners that to take all of Bougainville, with its garrison of about 40,000 Japanese in the northern tip,
near Buka airfield, and the southern tip, near Kahili,
would be exceptionally violent and costly. So it
was that Halsey elected to send the Marines in near
the island's center, at Empress Augusta Bay, beat
out a beachhead, and then establish a perimeter
inside which airfields could be constructed.

Bougainville, like Guadalcanal, was a tropical
pesthole, and the vicious land fighting was as brutal
as that on the Island. If anything, the climate—
wet—and the mud—glutinous—were worse. And
the Japanese soldier fought to the death.

On November 1, 1943, while troops of the 3rd

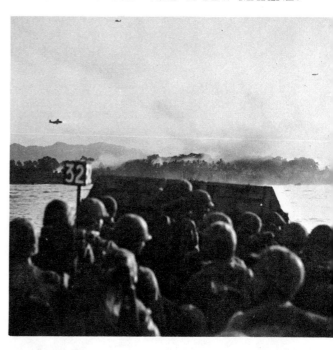

*Under the cover of Marine Avengers, the Marines head
for the beaches of Bougainville, Solomon Islands, November 1, 1943.* (DEFENSE DEPT., MARINE CORPS)

Marine Division and the 2nd Raider Regiment
splashed ashore at Cape Torokina on Empress Augusta Bay, Avengers and Dauntlesses swooped in
low to strafe and bomb the beachhead. Navy and
Marine planes patrolled over the area in anticipa-
tion of the reaction from the several nearby Japanese air bases. This came minutes before the first
barge ground upon the beach. About thirty Zekes
and bombers converged upon Torokina to be chal-
lenged by the P-40s of the New Zealand Royal Air
Force's No. 18 Squadron, the P-38s of the U. S.
Air Force's 18th Fighter Group, as well as Navy
and Marine Wildcats and Corsairs. In the first skirmish Captain James E. Swett, returned to VMF-
221 after his dip in the sea, shot down two Vals
besides sending a Tony (the Kawasaki Ki. 61
Hien), one of the newer Japanese fighters, smoking
away from the beachhead and off the tail of one of
the New Zealand P-40s.

In this initial encounter with the Japanese opposition to the Bougainville landings, seven of their
aircraft were lost, with no losses by the Allies.

In the early afternoon, during the patrol of VMF-
215—five Corsairs led by Lieutenant Colonel Her-

Bougainville-based Avenger takes off the island's air-strip on a bombing mission. Avengers were used by *Marines as torpedo and regular bombers.*
(DOUGLAS WHITE/DEFENSE DEPT., MARINE CORPS)

bert H. Williamson—a large formation of Japanese bombers and fighters came in to strike the ships and troops now cluttering up the shore line of the beaches at Torokina. Williamson led his Corsairs down upon the enemy bombers and a confused battle developed.

Flying with VMF-215 was one of the most colorful Marine pilots of the war, Lieutenant Robert M. Hanson, son of Methodist missionaries from Massachusetts. Hanson had been born in India in 1920 and had been a Marine flyer since February 1943. In the battle of the afternoon of the Bougainville landings, Hanson singlehandedly attacked six Kates with such ferocity that several jettisoned their bombs before reaching Torokina. Three others fell in flames under Hanson's guns (two others were knocked down by other men of VMF-215). But a rear gunner in one of the Kates shot down Hanson.

Setting his Corsair down on the water, Hanson broke out his dinghy and sat in it awaiting further developments. For nearly six hours Hanson waited until he saw the destroyer *Sigourney*, on its way back to Vella Lavella to pick up more passengers

for Torokina. Alternately waving and paddling, Hanson set out for the *Sigourney* cheering himself with the Cole Porter song "You'd Be So Nice to Come Home To." The American ship veered slightly from course, picked up the redoubtable Marine, and continued on to Vella Lavella.

Upon returning to VMF-215 Hanson continued with his nonchalant spree of destruction. In one period of seventeen days he shot down twenty enemy aircraft, which earned him the nickname of "Butcher Bob." Four of these victories were achieved on January 30, 1944, during an Avenger strike on Rabaul. Hanson flew with the escort and during the battle over the great Japanese base, now within easy reach of the base at Torokina, shot down four of the twenty-one Japanese planes destroyed during the mission. This brought his total of Japanese planes destroyed up to twenty-five.

Three days later, on February 3, the day before Hanson's twenty-fourth birthday and a week before he was scheduled to return to the United States, Hanson volunteered for a strafing mission in the Rabaul area, upon Cape Saint George, New Ireland. On this point, across the channel from New

Robert M. Hanson, whose way with a Japanese plane earned him the name of "Butcher Bob" at Bougainville. (DOUGLAS WHITE/DEFENSE DEPT., MARINE CORPS)

Gregory "Pappy" Boyington, "AWOL" Flying Tiger and leader of the Marine's raffish "Black Sheep" (VMF-214). (DEFENSE DEPT., MARINE CORPS)

Britain, stood a lighthouse which afforded the Japanese a fine lookout. Though never actually destroyed, it was a bothersome, challenging target. Hanson came in low over the cape and never came out of his run. Apparently hit by antiaircraft guns, Hanson crashed into the sea ending one of the most meteoric fighter pilot careers in the Pacific.

Until he was killed, it appeared that Hanson would equal or even surpass the score of another doughty Marine, Major Gregory Boyington, who had himself been splashed into the Pacific over Rabaul a month before Hanson was lost. Boyington's record (which included his Flying Tiger tally also) stood at twenty-eight (two reported after the war) enemy planes when he went down on January 3, 1944. After an extensive search Boyington was listed as "missing in action."

This, like his "desertion" and subsequent dishonorable discharge from the Flying Tigers, was an exaggeration. Although his wingman, Captain George

M. Ashmun, had been killed during the bitter fighting over Rabaul, Boyington had succeeded in parachuting from his burning Corsair. He dropped into Saint George Channel, off Rabaul, and was worked over for about a quarter of an hour by four strafing Zekes. Although unhit, Boyington was taken prisoner by a submarine which surfaced near him and he spent the rest of the war as a celebrity prisoner, although not an especially well-treated one.

A stanch individualist, Boyington (called "Pappy" by his men because of his advanced age of thirty-one) had returned to the Marines after he had bid a not too fond farewell to the Flying Tigers. While he rankled under discipline and adhering to the book, he was a born flyer and a unique leader. He may not have fitted into the organization of a squadron, but he could lead one. In recognition of this he was given permission to organize his own unit of misfits, appropriately dubbed "the Black Sheep" but more formally Marine Fighter Squadron 214

Tending his flock: Boyington briefs his Black Sheep before a fighter sweep over Rabaul; Boyington was *listed as Missing in Action after one of these sweeps and remained a prisoner of war for the duration.*

(MARINE CORPS)

(VMF-214). This occurred after a couple of fairly uneventful tours by Boyington in the Solomons.

When Bougainville's airstrips were sufficiently secure, Major General Ralph J. Mitchell, Marine commander of the aerial operations in the Solomons, instituted the first harassing fighter sweeps over Rabaul. The first of these—December 17, 1943—in which Boyington participated consisted of no less than seventy-six planes (twenty-three New Zealand P-40s of Nos. 14 and 16 Squadrons, twenty-two of the new Grumman F6F "Hellcat," and thirty-one Corsairs). With this formidable array of air power, the Japanese were not anxious to take off despite Boyington's profane invitations to "come up and fight."

"Come on down, sucker," was the Japanese answer. And the only fighting occurred at the P-40 level, which cost three of these, including that of New Zealand Wing Commander Freeman; however, the New Zealanders got five Japanese planes and

the Americans two. But it was not worth the effort, and upon his return Boyington argued that such a mixed bag of aircraft (all with different performances) and so unwieldy a number simply did not work.

Boyington believed in smaller, more flexible, and better-matched formations—which he got for future fighter sweeps upon Rabaul, as well as for escort missions with bombers. This was found to be more efficient, and Boyington's Black Sheep scored heavily against the Zekes. Between the first strike of December 17 and the first of the New Year, fighter sweeps over Rabaul claimed nearly 150 Japanese planes shot out of the air (after the war the Japanese admitted to 64).

Rabaul by early 1944 was in serious trouble. As new airstrips were completed on Bougainville, even short-range medium bombers could make the round trip to Rabaul. Before long, too, Thirteenth Air Force Mitchells based on Stirling Island (in the

Treasury group south of Bougainville) were reaching the beleaguered base. It was by no means out, as General Kenney rather prematurely claimed in early November 1942, but it was becoming more and more untenable for both shipping and aircraft.

Hoping to hold off the inevitable (which the Japanese believed meant an American invasion of Rabaul), Koga sent the air groups of the 2nd Koku Sentai (Carrier Division), under Rear Admiral Takaji Jojima, to bolster up the 26th Koku Sentai (in this instance, Air Flotilla—that is, land-based Navy planes). Late in January 1944 about 130 aircraft arrived from Truk to bring the total of planes at Rabaul up to the 300 mark. But it was to no avail as the massive American air power grew. Japanese pilots, long stationed at Rabaul, were worn, tired, and dispirited. It seemed that American planes came over almost at will, not only to bomb but to strafe the gun positions.

Just such a mission fell to the Bougainville-based Navy squadron, VF-17, which had arrived on January 24, the day before the planes of the 2nd Koku Sentai landed at Rabaul. On February 19, after several days of grueling operations, VF-17 was scheduled for an early morning strafing attack upon gun positions around Rabaul. Of the twenty Corsairs assigned to the job, sixteen were to concentrate upon the AA installations and the newly arrived Zekes and Tonys at Lakunai airfield. The four other Corsairs were assigned top cover, which was led by Lieutenant Merle Davenport.

The twenty Corsairs rose into a beautifully clear, sunlit sky. Climbing to about seventeen thousand feet, the Navy planes pushed onward toward New Britain. As the outline of the island emerged sharply from the glittering sea, Lieutenant Ira C. Kepford noticed that something appeared to be wrong with the Corsair of his wingman, Ensign Donald McQueen. It flew erratically and spouted puffs of smoke from the cowling. Closing in he saw that McQueen was having engine trouble—a common malady, thanks to the fine coral dust which abounded on Bougainville. McQueen must turn back, and so must Kepford, for without a wingman he could not participate in the raid on Rabaul. But Lieutenant Commander Roger Hedrick, commander of VF-17, ordered McQueen back to base and granted Kepford permission to continue with the formation until they arrived over Rabaul. There

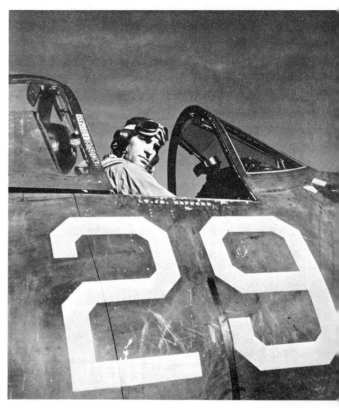

Ira C. Kepford, Corsair pilot of Navy Squadron VF-17, based at Bougainville.
(NAVY DEPT., NATIONAL ARCHIVES)

seemed little possibility of McQueen's being attacked on his flight back to Bougainville.

Scanning the sky and convinced that it was clear, Kepford pulled up alongside Davenport's plane and, dipping the Corsair's gull wings, blew a kiss to Davenport and his wingman and made a wide turn for the flight back to base. Reluctant to leave, Kepford deliberately made a ranging turn as he studied the Japanese positions below. Suddenly he saw a black object in the sky approaching him. As it came closer he recognized it as a float plane (a Rufe) and swept in for the kill. The Rufe pilot, unaware of the presence of the lone Corsair, soon was sent down into the water.

Having followed the Japanese plane to make certain it had crashed, Kepford again climbed to resume his flight back to Bougainville. In the distance, high above and closer to Rabaul, Kepford spotted more dots—as he counted them he realized they were Zekes, more than fifty, waiting to pounce on Davenport and the Corsairs at seventeen thousand feet. Kepford radioed the information to Davenport, hoping that he had not yet been seen by the Japanese planes. He hugged the waves and hoped, but not for long. Four fighters, two Zekes and two of the new Tojos, dived out of the big formation to take care of the lone stray.

When they came within range the enemy fighters opened up on the Corsair. Thinking fast, Kepford suddenly "popped his flaps," which caused the Corsair to slow down abruptly, and the lead Zeke overran him. As it pulled up to turn, Kepford shot away most of its tail surfaces and the Zeke pilot, discouraged, left the battle. The two Tojos (the fast Nakajima Ki. 44 *Shoki*) came in from the right and the remaining Zeke closed in from the left. Apparently the Japanese pilots were trying to force Kepford to head north instead of south. His Corsair had just been equipped with an emergency water-injection system which, when applied, charged the engine with a great surge of power for a limited time.

This, Kepford reasoned, was an emergency: all but boxed in by three enemy fighters far from home base. He rammed in full throttle and activated the water injection and began to outstrip the Zeke and even the faster Tojos. The Corsair ran out of energy over the western shore of New Ireland—the enemy planes had driven Kepford to the north—and he was still far from home. In desperation he eased back on the throttle and injected water again. Once again the Corsair responded and the plane shot ahead. Though the three planes continued to pursue him, they were not putting any holes in him.

The chase continued at close to four hundred miles an hour, very near the surface of the sea. Kepford saw that his fuel was getting low and his emergency spurts had been consumed; the engine complained after the injection. He must move quickly. The Zeke was still close behind him. Kepford suddenly kicked left rudder and the Corsair whipped quickly to the left as Kepford's blood drained in the turn. His vision faded under the pres-

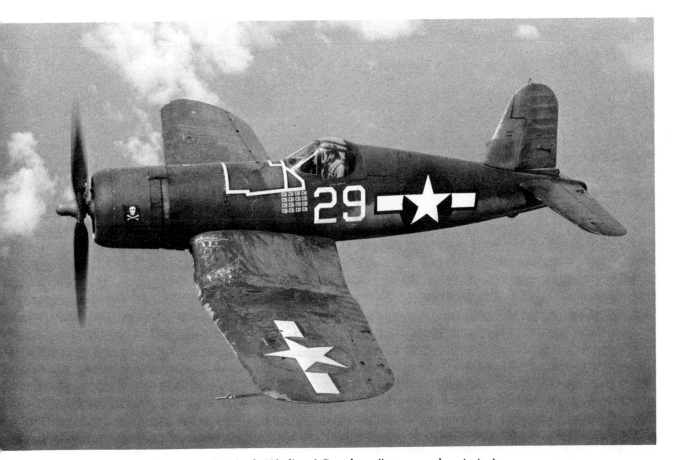

The battle-scarred Corsair of Ira Kepford; "Skull and Crossbones" was squadron insignia.

(NAVY DEPT., NATIONAL ARCHIVES)

A Corsair comes in for a landing on the Bougainville strip, constructed of linked steel matting over sand.

A C-47 is ready for takeoff. In the distance, below Corsair, a barrage balloon floats limply.
(P. SCHEER/DEFENSE DEPT., MARINE CORPS)

sure of the turn, but he managed to keep from blacking out completely.

The Zeke had followed with terrifying persistence and as Kepford's vision returned he saw the guns sparkling in the wing of the enemy plane. But at the same time the Zeke had attempted to turn more sharply, inside the Corsair's turn. As a wing dipped in the turn, the Zeke's wing tip brushed the water. There was a small splash, and then a series of big ones as the Japanese fighter cartwheeled across the surface of the water until its wings ripped off and it sank into the sea.

Anxiously Kepford looked back to see what became of the Tojos, but they had been lost in the turn and no longer continued the chase.

Despite the great consumption of fuel during the emergency use of the water-injection system, Kepford, though shaken, managed to return to Bougainville. He emerged from his shot-up Corsair bathed in perspiration, shaking with shock and with tears streaming down his face. A shot of brandy and nearly twenty-four hours of sleep restored the future Navy ace (with a total of seventeen victories he was the fifth-ranking ace in the U. S. Navy). The water-injection emergency system was widely

adopted and undoubtedly, as it did Kepford's, saved many an American airman's life.

On February 20, the day following Kepford's encounter, Rabaul was all but abandoned by the Imperial Navy. The 2nd Koku Sentai was pulled out and what remained of it returned to Truk, now the main Japanese base in the Pacific. Within days Allied bombers flew over the once hazardous area without escort. Rabaul, the formidable, became a milk run.

By March 6, 1944, the Green Islands, north of Bougainville and only 115 miles east of Rabaul, were occupied U. S. Marines and New Zealand troops. MacArthur's forces had already taken Cape Gloucester on New Britain itself. When Emirau Island, ninety miles north of the chief Japanese air base at Kavieng in New Ireland, was taken in April of 1944, it bottled up Rabaul completely. Invasion of Rabaul was unnecessary. Those Japanese troops stranded there were not going to do anything, nor were they going anywhere. Isolated, the Japanese troops remained there until the war ended, harassed continually by bombardment and the demoralizing realization that they wasted away ineffectually on another worthless island.

The ring closing in around Rabaul; Thirteenth Air Force Mitchells have just bombed a supply dump at Rataval. Simpson Harbour and Rabaul lie in the distance. (U. S. AIR FORCE)

Rabaul checkmate: as surface ships carry troops to occupy Green Island, B-25s head for Rabaul to occupy Japanese air power during the beachhead landings. The taking of Green Island neutralized Rabaul. No invasion was necessary. (U. S. AIR FORCE)

5

TURKEY SHOOT

F_{AR} to the north of the steaming, fevered Solomons lay another island chain of questionable worth. Though still in the Pacific, the string of islands called the Aleutians was in another world. The contrast between the Solomons and the Aleutians could hardly have been more extreme if, indeed, they had been on different planets. Many who served in each frequently wished they were.

The Japanese had invaded the Aleutians, setting troops ashore at two of the westernmost islands, Attu and Kiska, as a subsidiary action of the ill-fated Battle of Midway. They had lost the great naval-aerial battle in exchange for two tiny, inhospitable, wind-swept rocks. They also lost an almost intact Zero on one of the Aleutians close to the American base at Dutch Harbor. The sequel to this single mishap, in the form of the Grumman F6F "Hellcat" fighter in the summer of 1943, rendered the taking of Attu and Kiska extremely costly.

The proximity of these two islands to Alaska, and therefore to the North American mainland, made it imperative that the Japanese be driven off. On the other hand, the Japanese saw the Aleutians "pointing like a dagger at the heart of Japan," so that the islands—on a map in the hands of an armchair strategist, at least—took on great strategic significance. Depending on which side pushed the hardest, it appeared that the islands formed stepping-stones into the back yard of the other. This was

true, of course, provided the terrain and the weather could be nicely disregarded.

But to those who were there it was impossible. Admiral King stated the problem in his report to the Secretary of the Navy: "Since the Aleutian Islands constitute an aerial highway between the North American continent and the Far East, their strategic value is obvious. On the other hand, that chain of islands provides as rugged a theater for warfare as any in the world. Not only are the islands moun-

A snowbound Alaska-based Airacobra; with the Japanese in the Aleutians, the North Pacific became one of the most uncomfortable theaters of war and especially inimical to aerial operations. (U. S. AIR FORCE)

A P-40 based on Umnak Island (Aleutians); "Flying Tiger" markings are a tribute to the father of the pilot, Major John Chennault. (U. S. AIR FORCE)

tainous and rocky, but the weather in the western part of the islands is continually bad. The fogs are almost continuous, and thick. Violent winds (known locally as 'williwaws') with accompanying heavy seas make any kind of operation in that vicinity difficult and uncertain."

This was, as was characteristic of the cool King, true though understated. However, to the men of the Eleventh Air Force and the Navy's Patrol Wing 4 the Aleutians were no "aerial highway."

Nor were they an attractive spot for ships. As wryly put by Major General Simon B. Buckner, Jr., in charge of the Alaska Defense Command (which in turn, actually came under the command of the Navy in the person of Rear Admiral Robert A. Theobold), "the naval officer had an instinctive dread of Alaskan waters, feeling that they were a jumping-off place between Scylla and Charybdis and inhabited by a ferocious monster that was forever breathing fogs and coughing up 'williwaws' that would blow the unfortunate mariner into uncharted rocks and forever destroy his chances of becoming an admiral."

All operations in the Aleutians were circumscribed and dictated by nature, not man. Consequently assignment to the theater was more like being relegated to a frigid purgatory than to war. But operations did take place, whenever possible, as the Navy flew reconnaissance missions and the Air Force bombed the Japanese holdings at Attu and Kiska. "During April and May," an Air Force historian noted, "the weather for air operations is bad, during the rest of the year it is worse." Distance was another factor, for to reach Kiska, for example, the heavy bombers had to make a trip of twelve hundred miles from their base at Umnak. Bomb load would have to be sacrificed to fuel. Weather fore-

Mud, cold, fog—the conditions under which men and machines operated in the Aleutians. These Eleventh

Air Force Liberators have just returned from a bombing mission in the soup. (U. S. AIR FORCE) casts were meaningless, for in an instant a target was fogged over. The Aleutians war was one primarily of waste and frustration.

The Japanese shared these frustrations with the Americans, for air operations for them were equally difficult. The problem of supply was acute. In time, the Americans had hacked out bases on Adak and Amchitka islands, which were much closer to the Japanese-held islands than Umnak or Dutch Harbor. By March of 1943, although still a forgotten theater, the Japanese found that attempting to supply their garrisons in the Aleutians was hazardous. Naval ships and planes, Army Air Force bombers and fighters (the P-38s of the 54th Fighter Squadron and the P-40s of the 18th Fighter Squadron) made supply runs by Japanese surface ships nearly hopeless. Even so, they remained.

Although not wishing to transform the northern Pacific into a major theater of operations and therefore complicating the priorities for the other theaters, notably North Africa and the warmer reaches of the Pacific, the Joint Chiefs of Staff agreed that the Japanese should be knocked out of Attu. At the same time Kiska, which was more heavily occupied, could be bypassed and cut off from the Japanese bases in the Kurile Islands. This idea, put forward by Admiral Kinkaid, in command of the North Pacific Force, seemed feasible and was put into operation.

The two Japanese garrisons were bombed as frequently as weather permitted, by the Eleventh Air Force B-24s as well as by P-38 and P-40 fighter bombers. Finally, in May 1943, the 7th Infantry Division went in to take Attu from the Japanese. This is a simple statement, but taking Attu was no

Mission's end: after bombing Japanese positions in the Aleutians, this B-24 found its own home base socked *in with fog and had to find a soft landing spot nearby in a smooth tundra.* (U. S. AIR FORCE)

The new Yorktown *in the Pacific. The great carrier's keel was laid six days before Pearl Harbor and it was launched on January 21, 1943. Commissioned in April, the* Yorktown *(named for the ship that went down at Midway) began operations in the Pacific by August. The earliest combat experience was gained by strikes upon Japanese-held islands such as Marcus, Wake, the Gilberts, Kwajalein.*

(NAVY DEPT., NATIONAL ARCHIVES)

simple task. From May 11 through the thirtieth, besides contending with the cold (the division had been trained with typical military wisdom in California) and the weather, the men of the 7th Division fought an outnumbered but ferocious enemy. The fighting came to a horrible close with a shrieking banzai attack, and when that failed, the survivors committed suicide by putting hand grenades to their heads.

From Attu it was possible to bomb Japanese bases in the Kuriles, at the northern extremity of the Japanese home islands. Also it was possible to pound Kiska. The loss of Attu and the bombing of Kiska,

plus good common sense, eventually decided the issue. Even as American plans were under way to invade Kiska, the Japanese under cover of a period of heavy fog evacuated all of their troops from that unfriendly island. When the landings were finally made, the American and Canadian infantrymen found an eerie welcome: no Japanese; only three yellow dogs.

When troops entered what had been the Japanese command hut at Kiska they found a message scrawled on the wall: "We shall come again and kill out separately Yanki jokers." But they did not come again and the "Yanki jokers" were left with the world's worst weather, tundra, muskeg, and fog.

II

The Central Pacific, after the Battle of Midway, lay in a deceptive tranquillity for more than a year. While the fighting raged to the south and west (and later in the north), the forces and materials were slowly accumulated for the Central Pacific sweep toward Japan. What resources—men and matériel—could be spared from the European theater, where by the summer of 1943 the Allies had invaded Italy, went into the planning for the Central Pacific offensive.

Thus a great fleet, the Fifth, was organized under command of Vice-Admiral Raymond A. Spruance to spearhead the assault. The steel point of this head was no less than eleven carriers, including the new *Yorktown* and *Lexington,* both heavy carriers, replacing the older carriers. Also recently commissioned were the *Essex* and the *Bunker Hill.* Added to these were the veteran *Saratoga* and *Enterprise.* Five light carriers, all recently launched, were the *Independence, Princeton, Belleau Wood, Monterey,* and *Cowpens.* These were not all. For also to be employed in the operation ahead were eight escort carriers (the CVEs), smaller than the light carriers and designed to participate in close support of amphibious landings. In all, the Fifth Fleet had about nine hundred planes under its control for its assault into the Gilberts, Marshalls, and Marianas.

Preliminary strikes were made upon Tarawa and Makin (in the Gilberts) by carrier planes beginning on November 13, 1943; diversionary attacks were also made upon Wake and Marcus islands to the north. That this succeeded in confusing the Japanese as to where the next American assault would come was obvious. Admiral Koga sent Ozawa's Third Air Fleet (Koku Kantai) and Kurita's Second Air Fleet to the Marshalls, expecting the first heavy blow to fall there. When that did not come, he had nothing else to do (besides wonder) but return the planes to Rabaul.

The B-24s of the Seventh Air Force—originally based in Hawaii—began flying long-distance bombing missions to the Gilberts and Marshalls. The Seventh Air Force opened up its chapter in the Central Pacific offensive when on November 13, 1943, nine Liberators of its 431st Squadron (which was based on Funafuti in the Ellice Islands, south of the Gilberts) bombed Tarawa Atoll. Other units of the Seventh were based upon several other islands: Nanomea and Nukufetau (also in the Ellices) and Canton in the Phoenix Islands. Besides two B-24 squadrons at Canton, there were also two fighter squadrons, one of P-40s and the other of P-39s. These were stationed alongside the A-24s of the 531st Fighter Bomber Squadron. Another fighter squadron was stationed at Baker Island, a forward base, east of the Gilberts and north of the Ellices. This was to function as a staging area for fighters and a port in a storm for crippled bombers.

The Seventh Air Force, as can be seen, was dispersed over, in its own phrase, "one damned island after another."

This might very well have summed up the emotions of Admiral Mineichi Koga as he tried to decide, during the spring of 1943, where the next full-scale allied assault would fall. His head must have swirled under the widespread attacks; only strikes to begin with, but an indication of what was in the offing. His predecessor, Yamamoto, had been right. Given time, the great American productive potential would uncoil like a massive spring. Soon it would be reaching for the big base at Truk.

All doubts were cleared up when troops of the American 27th Infantry Division began coming ashore at Makin in the Gilberts on November 20, 1943. The next day Marines of the 2nd Division stormed the beaches of Tarawa. By November 24 the Army commander could claim small literary immortality by announcing "Makin taken"; but the Marines on Tarawa were destined to fight one of their most savage battles over the same period of time. Makin was lightly held, but Tarawa was not. The Air Force and carrier plane bombings had not softened up the Japanese positions. And although the pre-invasion naval bombardment was hoped to finish the job (it was more massive than aerial bombings), it did not penetrate the coconut log, concrete, and coral sand emplacements. The Navy, experiencing its first large-scale amphibious operation, miscalculated the degree of bombardment these Japanese fortifications could withstand. The prize of Tarawa was the airfield on Betio Island.

Rear Admiral Keiji Shibasaki with 4836 picked troops of Imperial Marines under his command, and the knowledge that fifteen months of burrowing and building had gone into the island's defenses, boasted that "a million Americans could never take the island in a thousand years."

He was, of course, wrong, for a considerably lesser number secured the island in about three days. The cost was high: nearly 1000 Marines died (of a total of 3301 casualties) and nearly all of Shibasaki's crack troops were wiped out (4690 killed out of a force of 4836). The admiral himself was buried, possibly still alive, in one of his nearly impregnable bombproof shelters by Marine bulldozers. Gasoline, poured into air vents, and hand grenades did the rest.

Aerial operations during the Gilberts battle were shared among the various groups of Task Force 50, commanded by Rear Admiral Charles A. Pownall. (Land-based aircraft were assigned to Task Force 57, but these too came ultimately under Navy control.) Task Group 50.1 (built around the *Yorktown, Lexington,* and *Cowpens*) operated in the area between the Marshalls and the Gilberts to interfere with any attempt by the Japanese to reinforce the Gilberts during the operations there. Carrier planes were engaged principally in attacks upon Japanese airfields on Mili and Jaluit in the Marshalls.

Task Group 50.2 (the *Enterprise, Belleau Wood,* and *Monterey*) was assigned to the Northern Assault Force, which took Makin. Task Group 50.3 (the *Essex, Bunker Hill,* and *Independence*) supported the Betio landings. Another group, 50.4 (the *Saratoga* and *Princeton*), after attending to the airfield on Nauru Island, west of the Gilberts, operated later to the southwest of Tarawa as a relief group.

At first Japanese air reaction was light. The Solomons campaign had taken a heavy toll of the carrier-

Carrier strike on Wake Island as the Fifth Fleet ranged through the Central Pacific freely, confuting the Japanese. Wake, which had fallen on Christmas Eve 1941, a symbol of American defeat in the Pacific, was struck repeatedly by carrier planes although not invaded. Isolated, its original strategic importance dwindled. As the Dauntless pilot prepares to make his bomb run, smoke may be seen rising from what had been Camp Two (center, across lagoon) on Wake itself.

(NAVY DEPT., NATIONAL ARCHIVES)

A Seventh Air Force Liberator begins the softening up for the projected Marshalls campaign. The B-24 is about to turn on its bomb run for Wotje. Other islands in the group: Kwajalein and Eniwetok.

(U. S. AIR FORCE)

Deck landing accident aboard the Enterprise *en route to the Marshalls, November 1943. The Hellcat has veered off the flight deck and caught fire. Catapult* *officer, Lieutenant Walter Chewning, with one foot on the belly tank, climbs onto the wing to assist the pilot.*
(NAVY DEPT., NATIONAL ARCHIVES)

based aircraft; so had the battling in the New Guinea area. The Betio airfield was secured before Japanese air attacks materialized on the night of November 25.

That the Japanese were planning counterattacks was demonstrated early in the morning of the twenty-fifth. A submarine had slipped into the ship concentration and put a torpedo into the escort carrier, *Liscombe Bay,* some twenty miles off Makin. The first inkling of this was noted by the men aboard the other ships when they heard an explosion and then "a few seconds after the first explosion, a second explosion which appeared to come from inside the *Liscombe Bay* burst upward, hurling fragments and clearly discernible planes two hundred feet or more in the air [burning bits of metal and other debris fell on the decks of a destroyer five thousand yards away]. The entire ship seemed to explode and almost at the same instant the interior of the ship . . . glowed with flame like a furnace." In twenty minutes the *Liscombe Bay,* the first of its type to be lost, sank, taking 644 of its crew, including Rear Admiral H. M. Mullinnix and Captain I. D. Wiltsie, with it.

Search planes and torpedo planes immediately launched from the *Enterprise* found no trace of submarine I-175 which had sunk the little carrier.

That night the air hummed overhead with the sound of engines as Japanese "snooper" planes sought the American ships. A flare blossomed over the ships as radar-directed guns scanned skyward. It was near daylight on the ships, but the sky, except for the radarscopes, was screened in night. This was a prelude, as it had been at Guadalcanal: snoopers illuminated the target area with flares and the bombers followed. But no bombs came that first night, perhaps because the radar-controlled guns of the *North Carolina* discouraged the bombers, or because no real attack had been planned.

Something was afoot, obviously, for the next day snoopers poked around the edges of radar screens as soon as the sun dipped. Aboard the *Enterprise* counterplans were being discussed to deal with the clearly impending night attack.

Newly arrived aboard the *Enterprise* to command its Air Group 6 fighters was Lieutenant Commander Edward H. O'Hare, Medal of Honor recipient. Butch O'Hare had singlehandedly saved the *Lexing-*

Edward "Butch" O'Hare, Medal of Honor winner, who had singlehandedly saved the Lexington *by destroying or driving off nine Japanese bombers.*

ton off Bougainville in February 1942 by breaking up an attack by nine Japanese bombers. At that time O'Hare flew the F4F Wildcat; his new aircraft aboard the *Enterprise* was the F6F Hellcat, the plane specifically designed to fight the Zero. It was the plane which the lost Zero of the Aleutians had inspired. The Hellcat was tougher, faster, and a better high-altitude fighter than the Zeke. The lighter Japanese plane continued to be more maneuverable, but it paid for it by flaming all too readily, by lack of armor protection for the pilot, and by a comparatively flimsy construction which under the six 50s of the Hellcat all but disintegrated.

The Hellcat had been in action since August 31, 1943, when VF-5 of the *Yorktown* flew it in a carrier strike on Japanese installations on Marcus Island; VF-9 of the *Essex* was also equipped with the

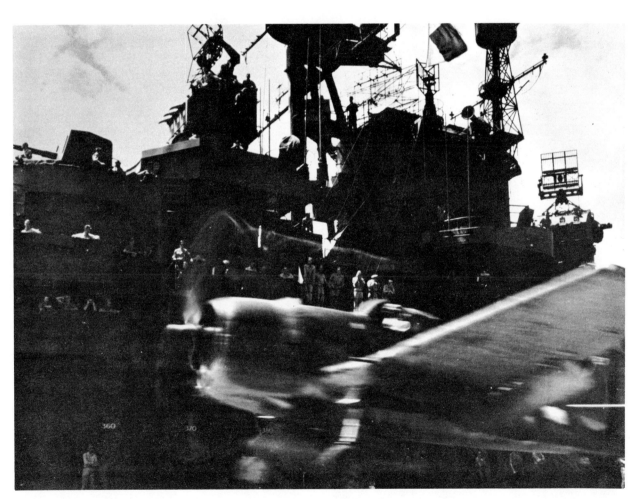

An F6F "Hellcat," the aircraft specifically designed to vanquish the Zero, taking off from the deck of a carrier. This is one of the hundreds of fine Navy photographs taken by, or under the supervision of, photographer *Edward Steichen (a Navy captain during the war).*

The toughness of the Hellcat is revealed in this photograph of one which has returned to its carrier after combat. Flames inside the fuselage have shriveled the skin; fire pours out of the flaps. Soon after, the pilot was rescued by shipmates and, though burned, survived the incident. (NAVY DEPT., NATIONAL ARCHIVES)

Poised on the flight deck, this Avenger gets the flag for takeoff. (U. S. NAVY)

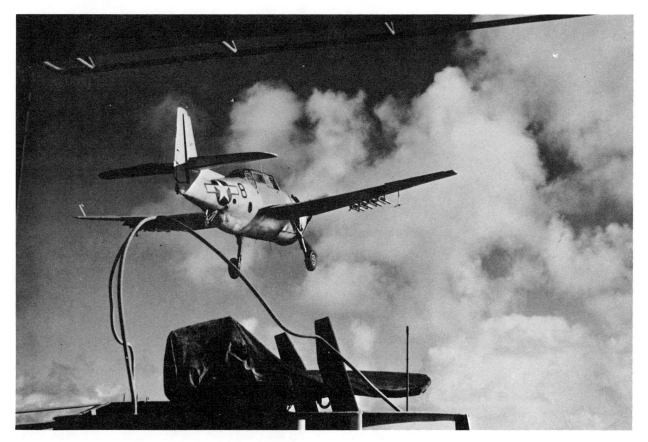

A rocket-armed Avenger springs into the air. Rockets were used in the Atlantic against German submarines and in the Pacific against Japanese shipping.

(U. S. NAVY)

Hellcat and participated in this strike. But it was during the Gilbert campaign that the Hellcat saw its first real action.

The planners of the *Enterprise,* however, had something else in mind for the coming night. If a radar-equipped Avenger could lead a Hellcat into the proximity of a Japanese bomber, the Hellcat could do the rest. That evening at dusk O'Hare took off with his wingman, Ensign Warren Skon, in their Hellcats. They were followed by an Avenger piloted by Lieutenant Commander John Phillips, *Enterprise* bomber leader. In the Avenger were also radar operator Lieutenant Hazen Rand and gunner A. B. Kernan. At the same time the large radar set in the Combat Information Center would track both the friendlies and the bogies.

The bogies came and went but little happened until Phillips was directed from the *Enterprise* toward enemy aircraft. O'Hare and Skon could not find the Avenger in the dark, let alone an enemy plane. Phillips meanwhile had the bogie on his own screen and with Rand guiding him came upon a Betty heading for the ships.

Three miles away O'Hare and Skon were startled to see a sudden flare in the sky. It fell burning into the water, forming a burning lake in the blackness. Other Bettys in the Japanese formation, surprised by the unexpected attack, began firing wildly at one another.

If that was where the action was, O'Hare and Skon turned and raced to the scene. Phillips meanwhile had been vectored onto another Betty. As he approached he heard O'Hare request that he turn on the navigation lights of the Avenger so that he and Skon could find him. Reluctantly Phillips flicked on the lights, which, as he had expected, alerted the Betty. But soon that bomber too went burning into the sea. Moments later, Kernan fired at a dark form passing near the Avenger's tail.

Under orders from the *Enterprise* all three American planes turned on their navigation lights to enable them to assemble. If there were enemy aircraft nearby this would of course place the Avenger and Hellcats in jeopardy. The two fighters moved in closer to the Avenger. Soon the two Hellcats overtook the Avenger, to their left. To better cover the larger plane, Skon throttled back, swooped under the tail, and took a position off the left wing of the Avenger. O'Hare slid back toward the right wing.

Suddenly Kernan's ball turret came to life, firing, according to his report, between the two Hellcats at a darkened plane approaching from the stern. The .50-calibers lighted up the night and then again there was darkness. O'Hare's Hellcat, with navigation lights still on, veered to the left and down. Skon, certain that O'Hare was attacking, followed, but the veer became a dive and the Hellcat disappeared into the night. All Skon's attempts to call his leader were fruitless, as were the searches made the next day by other aircraft. Butch O'Hare was gone. Although he may have been hit by a Japanese plane, it was more than likely that Kernan had hit him by mistake. It was a tragedy for Kernan (though not absolute, for there will always be the chance that a Japanese gunner shot O'Hare down) and the men of the *Enterprise*.

But then tragedy and error are the very ingredients of war. Six hundred men had died, too, in the *Liscombe Bay;* a thousand Marines lay dead on Tarawa alongside four times that number of Japanese. The death of one more airman increased the figure by a single digit. But it did not diminish the tragedy.

Tragedy multiplied becomes history, eliminating thus biography; and great numbers simply become symbols which stir the blood but only afflict the heart individually. Whatever the cost, Tarawa, Makin, and Abemama—the Gilberts—belonged to the Americans. The lessons learned there at so great a price would not be wasted.

III

The next step in the Central as well as South Pacific was defined at the so-called Sextant Conference in Cairo on December 3, 1943 (attended by Churchill, Roosevelt, and Chiang Kai-shek). Admiral King opposed the idea of relinquishing the Pacific war to MacArthur, submitting his own plan to the Allied Combined Chiefs of Staff for a dual approach in the Pacific. The Combined Chiefs concurred and issued their directive stating that the "advance along the New Guinea-Netherlands East Indies-Philippine axis will proceed concurrently with operations for the capture of the Mandated Islands. A strategic bombing force will be established in Guam, Tinian, and Saipan for strategic bombing of Japan proper." For this final phase a new bomber, the Boeing B-29 Superfortress, was being delivered to combat-training units in the United States.

The step between the Marianas (Guam, Saipan, and Tinian) was the Marshalls campaign. It proved to be one of the most successfully handled of the early combined operations, "characterized," in the words of Admiral King, "by excellent planning and by almost perfect timing in the execution of those plans." The experience gained in the Gilberts was not lost in the planning of the Marshalls invasions. As soon as the Seventh Air Force could begin launching bombing missions from new bases in the Gilberts the initial softening up of the targets began. With D-Day set for January 31, 1944, the carriers moved in two days before to strike at Majuro, Roi, and Kwajalein (in the Kwajalein Atoll), Taroa and Wotje. In concert with the Navy attacks, the Seventh Air Force sent over its B-24s and B-25s to harass the Japanese and to keep them off balance.

Japanese antiaircraft guns took their toll, but fighter defenses were weak because so many planes had previously been destroyed on the ground. Snoopers seemed even more timid than in the Gilberts. Then around dusk of January 29 the sudden appearance of nine planes low on the water electrified the fleet. The planes were quickly identified as twin-ruddered Nells and became the focus of destroyer antiaircraft guns. Combat air patrol Hellcats dropped down to attack the intruders also.

A trail of smoke came from one of the bombers before it splashed into the water. Loudspeakers on the American ships about then began booming, "Cease firing! Cease firing!" The planes that had been identified as Nells were, in fact, Mitchells of

---

Flaming Kate stopped by the gunners of the Yorktown *off Kwajalein, Marshall Islands, December 3, 1943.*
(NAVY DEPT., NATIONAL ARCHIVES)

the 820th Squadron (41st Bomb Group). The Mitchells had been on a mission to Wotje, where they were to have bombed shipping and shore installations. Coming in low over the water to avoid Japanese radar they had approached the unalerted Navy ships looking like torpedo bombers. The error cost the life of one man, injured five, and destroyed one Mitchell. Two others, seriously damaged, managed to return to Tarawa.

One by one, with almost clockwork precision, the islands fell: Majuro on January 31, Roi and Namur on February 2—but Kwajalein, the largest and strongest-held, took longer. Heavy shelling, much heavier than that which preceded the Tarawa landing, pounded the island for two days, almost up to the moment that the troops were put ashore. At nine-thirty in the morning of February 1, 1944, the Army's 7th Division (which had fought on Attu) began moving in. Like Tarawa, Kwajalein was ingeniously fortified and cluttered with tank traps, pillboxes, snarls of barbed wire, and trenches. The survivors of the weeks of bombing and the hours of shelling had to be rooted out, and, as before, the Japanese fought fanatically, almost heedlessly to the death. When the fighting ended all but the 35 Japanese who had surrendered were annihilated—close to 5000 men. The total cost of taking all of the Kwajalein Atoll was 372 soldiers and Marines; the Japanese lost 7870 men of 8675 which had garrisoned that atoll.

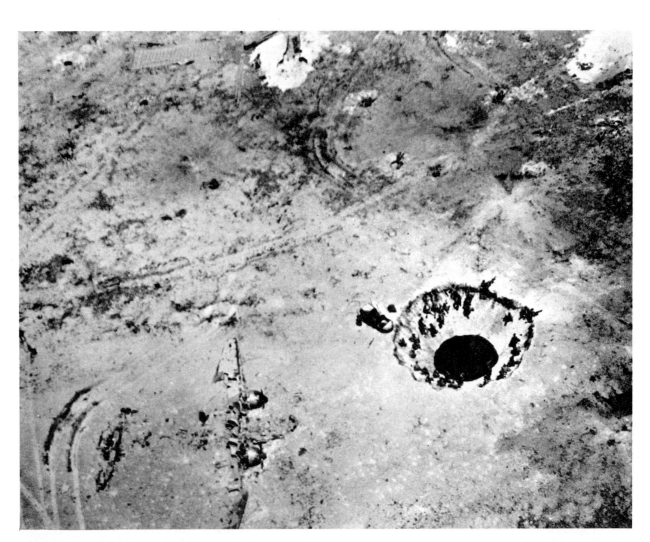

Eniwetok, Marshall Islands, under carrier plane attack. U. S. Marines take shelter in a shell hole as others set up machine guns (upper center); a burned out twin-engined Japanese bomber lies at bottom left.

(U. S. NAVY)

Navy Corsairs of the Intrepid *ready for a strike on Truk. Originally not regarded as suitable for carriers, the Corsair proved otherwise. These F4U-2s are* equipped with "radomes" near starboard wingtip for night operations. The Japanese hated this plane and called it "Whistling Death."

(NAVY DEPT., NATIONAL ARCHIVES)

When the taking of Majuro and Kwajalein had come off so smoothly, it was decided that one more of the Marshalls, Eniwetok Atoll, might be taken even earlier than had been originally planned. Set for May 10, D-Day on Eniwetok was moved up to February 17. This atoll lay about 325 miles west and north of Kwajalein and about 1000 miles from the Marianas. The pattern of softening up, bombardment, and assault was repeated, and by February 20 Eniwetok fell to American forces and the Marshall Islands belonged to the United States. Several of them—Jaluit, Mili, Maloelap, and Wotje (as was Nauru in the Gilberts)—were not invaded at all. They harbored Japanese troops, held air bases, but with the other positions in American hands these atolls were isolated from everything but American air and surface attacks.

During the Eniwetok assault, Truk, the vaunted "Gibraltar of the Pacific," Japan's most formidable base outside the home islands, was rendered almost neutral by the carrier planes of Rear Admiral Marc A. Mitscher's Fast Carrier Force. On the morning of February 17, after a surprisingly uneventful trip from Majuro in the Marshalls, a fighter sweep of seventy-two Hellcats pounced upon the air base at Truk. Fighting in the air cost four Navy planes, but the Japanese lost more than fifty in the air and even more on the ground. Avengers followed the fighters, planting incendiaries on the base, leaving behind less than a hundred operational planes with which the Japanese might contend the Eniwetok landings. Dive bombers destroyed the ships in the harbor, so that by February 18 Truk was no longer any kind of Gibraltar—and, in fact, was no longer even

Free riders: several Navy pilots came to grief near Truk during a carrier strike (April 30, 1944) due to Japanese antiaircraft or mechanical failures. This Kingfisher was sent to retrieve the dunked pilots and picked up so many—six from the Enterprise *and one from the* Langley—*that pilot John A. Burns could not take off.* (NAVY DEPT., NATIONAL ARCHIVES)

Truk. As "a formidable bastion" it was no more impressive, or potent, than any other bypassed island in the Pacific.

The Marshalls campaign closed with a carrier strike in the Marianas. Not since the fall of Guam (the largest and southernmost of the Marianas) in December 1941 had American planes passed over these islands. The purpose of the carrier raid was double: to cover the Eniwetok landings and to begin reconnaissance photography of Saipan, Tinian, Rota, and Guam for the proposed seizure of these islands for future bases. For the first time since the early Gilberts assaults, the Japanese attempted to fight back vigorously. As the carriers approached the Marianas the evening of February 21 was marked by heavy fighting.

Three attempts by bombers to stop the American ships were made by an estimated forty Japanese ships. Intense antiaircraft fire either shot them down

Last moments of a Japanese "Jill" (Nakajima B6N) torpedo bomber during an attempt at American ships off Truk. (NAVY DEPT., NATIONAL ARCHIVES)

or drove them off, and the armada, undamaged though zigzagging, continued westward to the morning's launch point. As at Truk, Hellcats swept in over the Japanese bases, strafing and burning. Aerial opposition by Japanese fighters, many already burned on the ground, was sporadic, tentative, and lacking in characteristic Japanese fatal determination. At the same time small ships in and around Saipan, Tinian, and Guam were strafed and bombed.

Japan's inner defense line, which ran through the Marianas, had been pierced. There was consternation in Tokyo and Admiral Koga, after ordering the fleet to evacuate Truk, hurried home to confer with the Imperial General Staff. The principal Japanese naval base was moved farther westward to Palau, practically on the doorstep of the Philippines. The defensive line was drawn from the Kuriles in the north, down past the home islands, through the Bonins, southerly through the Marianas, and westward to Palau. This line, Koga stated, must be held to the death. Palau lay across the path of MacArthur's forces hopping up the northern coast of New Guinea, as well as in the seas through which Halsey's ships moved toward Japan. And the Marianas, just to the northeast in the Philippine Sea, were also within reach.

American aircraft carriers became the main objective of Koga's plan, Order 73. He was fated never to know of the failure of this order, for on March 31,

The fighting in the Central Pacific intensifies; the American carriers have moved in close to Saipan, Mariana Islands, for a strike before the coming invasion. (NAVY DEPT., NATIONAL ARCHIVES)

1944, Koga was lost in a storm while flying from Saipan to Davao in the Philippines. He was succeeded by Admiral Soemu Toyoda, who like Yamamoto had opposed Japan's entry into war and was a realist besides, and, in the words of Samuel Eliot Morison, "a much more aggressive character," compared to Koga.

When he became Commander in Chief, Combined Fleet, Toyoda rather bluntly said, "The war is approaching areas vital to our national security. Our situation is one of unprecedented gravity. There is only one way of deciding this struggle in our favor."

The Americans must be stopped, once and for all, in the Marianas.

IV

As the Imperial Navy made preparations for an all-out effort to stop the enemy, Minister of the Army and Prime Minister General Hideki Tojo criticized the Navy's efforts as "hysterical" and refused to permit the use of Army aircraft in the Marianas. Toyoda could do nothing, then, but alert and deploy his naval forces. He would co-ordinate his carrier force, under command of Vice-Admiral Jisaburo Ozawa, with the land-based forces of Vice-Admiral Kakuji Kakuda. Kakuda's headquarters were on Tinian and his planes were deployed through the Marianas, the Carolines, Iwo Jima, and Truk—a total of about a thousand.

The Palau anchorage having been rendered unwholesome by the marauding American carriers, Ozawa awaited developments at Tawitawi, in the Sulu Sea, just west of the southern Philippines. Under Ozawa's command was the largest fleet assembled since the attack on Pearl Harbor: seventy-three ships, including nine carriers, among them the new heavy carrier *Taiho*. Never before in Japanese naval history had such a heavy concentration of battle planes been assembled. There were nearly 450 planes—Zekes, Kates, Vals, and the newer Nakajima *Tenzen* ("Jill") torpedo bomber and the not quite so new Yokosuka *Suisei* ("Judy") dive bomber. The latter two planes were designed to replace the aged Kate and Val.

To meet the rampaging American forces, Ozawa

had divided his aerial forces into three carrier divisions. The 1st, under his command, consisted of the three heavy carriers *Taiho* (the flagship), *Shokaku,* and *Zuikaku* (the two surviving veterans of the Pearl Harbor attack). Stationed aboard these carriers were the pilots of the 601st Kokutai (Air Corps). Rear Admiral Takaji Jojima commanded the 2nd Carrier Division: the light carriers *Hiyo, Junyo,* and *Ryuho,* carrying the 652nd Kokutai. The 3rd Carrier Division (Rear Admiral Sueo Obayashi) was assigned to the main body, which consisted also of battleships and cruisers which were to deal with the American fleet. Obayashi commanded the light carriers *Chiyoda, Chitose,* and *Zuiho* (653rd Kokutai). With so vast an accumulation of air power plus the assistance which might be expected from Kakuda's land-based planes, Japanese naval officers anticipated a great aerial slaughter of the Americans. This was planned to be finished by the battleships of Vice-Admiral Takeo Kurita's force, which included the great *Yamato* and *Musashi,* two of the world's most modern battleships. An exhilarating excitement gripped the young pilots as they waited impatiently for the word to leave Tawitawi.

Even these young, untried, inexperienced, and ill-trained warriors were inclined to a touch of "victory fever."

Only the veterans awaited the coming battle with reservations. The training of the pilots aboard the nine carriers, excepting a handful of experienced leaders, was tragically inadequate, ranging from as little as two months to a maximum of six. But lack of experience began at the top, for Ozawa had never taken part in a carrier battle. He was to oppose Rear Admiral Raymond A. Spruance, who had proved himself at Midway. Directly opposing Ozawa was Vice-Admiral Marc A. Mitscher's formidable Task Force 58. Mitscher not only had quality—better-trained men, better aircraft, his own battle shrewdness—on his side, he also had overwhelming, American-made quantity, as Yamamoto had foreseen.

Early in June 1944 Task Force 58 began its approach upon the southern Marianas. Only clichés could do it justice: "massive array of sea-air power," "the greatest armada ever assembled," for as "far as the eye could see"—and beyond—great, warlike ships churned through the Pacific. There were seven heavy carriers (the *Hornet, Yorktown, Bunker Hill,*

Task Force 58 "... the greatest armada ever assembled ..." in the summer of 1944 poised to move into the Marianas. (NAVY DEPT., NATIONAL ARCHIVES)

Wasp, Enterprise, Lexington, and *Essex*), eight light carriers (the *Bataan, Belleau Wood, Monterey, Cabot, San Jacinto, Princeton, Cowpens,* and *Langley*), seven new battleships, eight heavy cruisers, thirteen light cruisers, and sixty-nine destroyers. This does not include those ships directly assigned to Vice-Admiral Richmond K. Turner's amphibious forces, which would invade Saipan, then Guam, and then Tinian. Among the ships of Turner's force were several old battleships which had been damaged at Pearl Harbor, besides eight of the smaller escort carriers.

But before the landings could be made Mitscher's planes must begin clearing away Japanese aerial potential in and around Saipan. Leaving Majuro anchorage on June 6, 1944 (the same date but because of the International Date Line the day before the Normandy landings in Europe), Mitscher

put to sea. His carriers transported about double the number of aircraft Ozawa had on his carriers— over 890 planes, the bulk being Hellcats, plus Avengers, Dauntlesses, and the new Curtiss SB2-C "Helldiver." Pilots, incidentally, disdained the public relations name of the plane and preferred calling it simply the "2C."

According to plans, the amphibious forces, Marine and Army, would go ashore on Saipan on June 15. Three days before, Mitscher's carrier planes were to sweep over the Marianas airfields, bringing up the curtain on the operation. However, on the tenth Japanese air patrols spotted the approaching carriers; Toyoda, long suspecting, at last knew. Commander in Chief, Combined Fleet, had formulated his own plan: he hoped to lure the American fleet into the waters off the western Carolines (southwest of Guam). There, roughly in the vicinity of the Palau Islands and other Japanese bases (Yap and Woleai), with his vast aerial force he would annihilate the American carriers. Toyoda expected the

Island and flight deck of the Lexington *before Saipan.*

landings at Palau and tended to regard any Marianas operations as diversions masking MacArthur's New Guinea moves.

But Mitscher's main task was to prepare the way for and cover the landings in the Marianas; it would be difficult, however alluring, to entice him into the western Carolines. In fact, as soon as he realized that Japanese reconnaissance planes had found Task Force 58, Mitscher put on speed and steamed ahead for the Marianas. By the afternoon of June 11, though still about two hundred miles east of the Marianas, Mitscher launched his first fighter sweep —the Hellcats being guided to the targets by the better-equipped (in terms of navigational instruments) Avengers.

Although the Japanese had been aware of TF 58's presence, they were apparently preparing for the customary dawn attack for the next day. Also, undoubtedly, they were preparing for a snooper attack on the carriers that very evening. About two hundred Hellcats swarmed down upon Saipan, Tinian, and Guam, destroying planes on the ground and in the air. About 150 Japanese planes were erased from Kakuda's ground-based air forces in the Marianas, crippling all possible strong air retaliation. The first night off Saipan was free of Japanese attack.

The next day American destruction of airfields and other installations continued, and on the thir-

teenth the battleships started pounding the landing beaches. On this day, also, the Japanese fleet left Tawitawi and proceeded northward. Obviously the Americans intended to invade the Marianas (which had been the prediction of Commander Chikataka Nakajima of the Naval Intelligence Staff) and not Palau (as the Staff, in general, believed). Immediately canceled was Operation *Kon* (a plan to retake the importantly strategic island of Biak, off the northwest coast of New Guinea, which had fallen to MacArthur's forces), and Toyoda ordered Ozawa to proceed at full speed for Saipan—about two thousand miles away. At the same time Kakuda's land-based planes were ordered to hold off the Americans until Ozawa's forces arrived.

By this time about five hundred planes had been destroyed and with the remaining handful there was little resistance forthcoming, at least not from the air. On June 15 Marines and Army infantrymen (2nd and 4th Marine Divisions; 27th Infantry Division) struck the beaches of Saipan. They had been properly cautioned by Navy manuals and talks. The troops were warned to beware of sea life ringing the island: "sharks, barracuda, sea snakes, anemones, razor-sharp coral, polluted waters, poison fish and giant clams that shut on a man like a bear trap."

An officer read off, according to regulations, the joys of life ashore: leprosy, typhus, filariasis, yaws, typhoid, dengue fever, dysentery, saber grass, insects, snakes, and giant lizards.

"Eat nothing growing on the island," he continued reading; "don't drink its waters and don't approach the inhabitants." The End.

"Any questions?"

A hand was raised.

The officer nodded.

"Why don't we let them keep the island?"

Unlike Japanese Naval Intelligence, the young American Marine had never heard of the B-29. On Saipan, northernmost of the islands coveted by the Americans, the Japanese had constructed Aslito Field. At the northern end of the island—that is, opposite to the end on which Aslito lay—another airstrip was being set up. It was because of these air bases, primarily, that the Americans did not want the Japanese to keep the island, and for which the invading troops were expected to risk the nearly countless hazards of life in and around Saipan.

The invasion of Saipan, with carrier plane cover, begins; June 15, 1944. A Japanese ship burns near the shore. (NAVY DEPT., NATIONAL ARCHIVES)

Besides these natural perils there were Lieutenant General Yoshitsugo Saito's thirty thousand troops. Also on Saipan as Commander in Chief, Pacific Fleet, in command of all Japanese Marine and naval units in the area, was Vice-Admiral Chuichi Nagumo, the reluctant hero of Pearl Harbor. Nagumo agreed with others in the Japanese High Command: the Americans were aiming for Palau. Meanwhile Saito, grumbling because the Navy had lost supply ships and troop ships to American submarines, did the best he could to prepare "to destroy the enemy at the water's edge."

The day before the landings began Nagumo, having witnessed the aerial strikes of the previous four days, hedgingly proffered a prediction and a definition. "The Marianas are the first line of defense of our homeland. It is certain that the Americans will land in the Marianas group either this month or the next." They landed, of course, the next day.

During the Saipan invasion carrier sweeps over Guam to the south held down Japanese aerial intervention. On his mission Ensign A. P. Morner, Ironwood, Michigan, encountered six Zekes, shot down three, but was wounded himself and his Hellcat damaged—which resulted in this crash landing on Morner's home carrier. (U. S. NAVY)

Stowaways: Air Force Thunderbolts of the 318th Fighter Group (73rd Squadron) aboard the carrier Manila Bay. *Japanese Vals from Saipan contributed the splashes to port.* (U. S. AIR FORCE)

"Where are our planes?" lamented tank man Tokuzo Matsuya in a characteristic query. "Are they letting us die without making any effort to save us? If it were for the security of the Empire we would not hesitate to lay down our lives, but wouldn't it be a great loss to the Land of the Gods for us all to die on this island? It would be easy for me to die, but for the sake of the future I feel obligated to stay alive."

Marine Lieutenant General Holland M. Smith, in command of the ground troops for the invasion, found that "Saito met us at the beaches at Saipan in approved Japanese fashion, and our hopes of quickly expanding our beachhead were somewhat dampened. . . . The long twenty-five-day continuous attack against strongly entrenched and fiercely resisting troops on Saipan proved the most bitter battle in the Pacific up to that time." Intense mortar and artillery fire, plus suicidal, screaming night attacks by the Japanese, made life ashore dreadful and, for many, short. By June 18, however, Aslito Field fell to the Army's 27th Division. On June 22 Thunderbolts of the 19th and 73rd Squadrons of the 318th Fighter Group, catapulted from the es-

Thunderbolt of 73rd Squadron leaves deck of Manila Bay *for Aslito Field (renamed Isley Field), Saipan.* (U. S. AIR FORCE)

cort carriers *Manila Bay* and *Natoma Bay,* landed at Aslito to join the Navy planes already there. By this time the field was renamed Isley Field, in honor of Commander Robert H. Isley, commander of the *Lexington*'s torpedo planes. Two days before the Saipan landings Isley's Avenger was hit by antiaircraft fire over Aslito and crashed in flames onto the field itself. From Isley Field the Seventh Air

Aslito Field, Saipan, showing the ravages of American carrier plane attacks. Intact aircraft parked among the wrecks are U. S. Navy and Air Force planes.

(U. S. NAVY)

Force Thunderbolts engaged in close-support operations, a blasting away at Japanese positions in front of Marine and Army troops. Once established in the still beleagured airfield, the P-47s, when not engaged in sporadic air battles, bombed and strafed Japanese positions on Saipan and Tinian. By July, when the fighting on Saipan ended, the Thunderbolts of the 318th Fighter Group were armed with yet another weapon, at first popularly called the "fire bomb." These were the first of the frightfully effective napalm, diesel oil, and gasoline mixtures (later napalm and gasoline), which when dropped in wing and belly tanks from about fifty feet upon Japanese strong points (particularly caves) created a havoc of flame.

Meanwhile, even as American troops went ashore on Saipan, word was flashed from the submarine *Flying Fish* that a large Japanese carrier force had been sighted in San Bernardino Strait, headed for

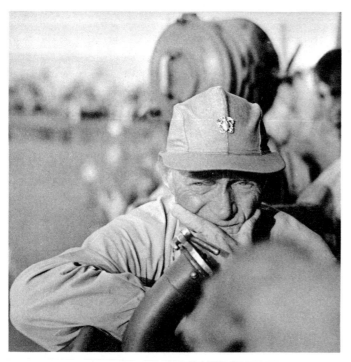

Marc Andrew Mitscher, USN, an early Navy air pioneer, canny air leader during Solomons campaign and commander of carrier force in the Central Pacific for the Marianas assault.

(NAVY DEPT., NATIONAL ARCHIVES)

the Marianas. The next day, June 16, *Seahorse,* another submarine, sighted more ships off Surigao Strait. Spruance knew then that the Combined Fleet was coming out in full force. He immediately canceled the proposed June 18 landing on Guam (although not the June 16 air strikes upon Iwo Jima in the Volcano Islands and Chichi Jima in the Bonins, south of the Japanese homeland).

American submarines, which were to play an important role in the impending "decisive battle," tracked the Japanese fleet, waiting for the moment when they might launch their fish. Spruance positioned his carriers by June 18 about 160 miles west of Tinian. On this same day—the day that Aslito Field fell—Ozawa's forces had arrived at a position about 500 miles west of Saipan. The opposing fleets by June 19 were about four hundred miles apart.

Ozawa, therefore, had the advantage. His planes, thanks to the lack of armor plating and the lack of the heavy self-sealing fuel tanks, enjoyed a greater range than the American carrier fighters. Even before his carriers came within range of the American

carriers—Ozawa's major targets—he could launch his planes, which, after combat, could land on the Marianas airfields (excepting, of course, Aslito). Japanese search planes, meanwhile, sought out the American fleet as the Japanese carriers made preparations to hurl total destruction upon Spruance's carriers.

June 19 dawned clear over the American carriers. The night before, the pilots had been disappointed because Spruance would not authorize Mitscher, in tactical command of the carriers, to speed westward to intercept the Japanese. Spruance had in mind that the primary mission of Task Force 58 was to cover the Saipan invasion. If the carriers were too far west, there was always a possibility of Japanese ships coming in to pound the Americans from the sea. Aboard the *Lexington,* his flagship, Mitscher was reported to have stalked into his sea cabin to blow off steam in private. On the *Enterprise* Captain Matthias B. Gardner, complying, said nothing but is reported to have "hurled down his hat and stomped on it." (Spruance was later criticized for holding his carriers near Saipan and not taking the offensive on June 18. Critics, however, ex post facto as usual, possessed certain vital information which at the time the Japanese were not bestowing upon Spruance.)

Mitscher's eager pilots, however, would not lack for action on the nineteenth. An early morning strike on Orote Field on Guam was mounted to keep that base neutralized in the event that the impending battle materialized. About thirty Wildcats pounced on the already beaten-up field; a rather surprising antlike activity seemed in progress as Japanese planes were pushed out of revetments and put into the air with frantic resolution. The Wildcats began the morning's decimation, shattering the Japanese planes, barely air-borne, out of the bright morning sky.

In about an hour and a half of fighting, the American combat air patrol shot down thirty-five of Kakuda's land-based planes, which had up to that morning escaped previous attacks. Meanwhile, tension aboard the carriers mounted as Mitscher wondered about the location of the Japanese carriers.

Ozawa had begun launching his planes at dawn, search planes and bombers (a total of seventy-three), which fanned out into a squally sky to look for the American fleet. The imperfect weather over

Hellcats of VFN-76 on the Lexington *near Saipan; radomes converted these planes into night fighters that* *dealt with Japanese night "snoopers," reconnaissance planes and bombers.*

the Japanese ships, stretching nearly to the American dispositions, was a disadvantage to the inexperienced Japanese pilots. Animated with patriotism and little else, they were led like strangely pugnacious sheep to slaughter. Ozawa's first raid, led by Lieutenant Commander Masayuki Yamagami, began taking off at daybreak and vanished into murky eastern sky. Then Ozawa waited. He could afford to, for his ships were still beyond the range of Mitscher's carrier planes.

He was determined to make a thorough job of the Americans, so even as the planes of the first raid were taking off the van carriers of the 3rd Carrier Division, the planes of the 1st Carrier Division began launching also. Forty-eight Zekes, fifty-four Judys, and twenty-seven Jills took off from the *Zuikaku, Shokaku,* and *Taiho.* From the bridge of the latter, Japan's great new carrier, Ozawa observed the air swarming with planes. The *Taiho* was a gigantic vessel of more than sixty-four thousand tons. Launched just three months before (April 4, 1944), the *Taiho* was considered unsinkable.

As the last plane left the deck of the flagship a torpedo track was discovered knifing through the water at the *Taiho.* Warrant Officer Sakio Komatsu, whose plane was in the last wave, saw the churning line in the water and died believing he had saved the flagship by diving into the torpedo, detonating it. But that was not the only "fish" which had been ejected from the torpedo tubes of the *Albacore,* an American submarine in the area (under command of J. W. Blanchard), and despite attempts to turn the *Taiho,* it was struck. The blow jammed an elevator and fuel piping ruptured, filling the hangar space below decks with fumes. A single spark did the rest, for within six hours the *Taiho* was ripped by a splintering explosion. A mass of flames from stem to stern, the *Taiho* turned over and sank.

Admiral Ozawa in the meantime had moved to another ship, the heavy cruiser *Haguro.* He was an unhappy man, for even while the *Taiho* reeked with impending doom yet another carrier was attacked—this time the *Skokaku,* which became the victim of Lieutenant Commander H. J. Kossler's submarine *Cavalla.* The *Shokaku* sank even before the *Taiho.*

Before these misfortunes, however, Ozawa had launched about four hundred planes in four attack waves. The first of these was detected by American radar when they were almost 150 miles away, at Guam. When the first blips of aircraft apparently approaching from the open sea appeared on the radar screens, it was Mitscher himself who took the microphone of the TBS (Talk Between Ships) and initiated what would come to be called the "Marianas Turkey Shoot."

"Hey, Rube!" echoed through the fleet, alerting

A Japanese plane shot aflame by antiaircraft fire from American ships attempts to crash into flight deck of escort carrier Sangamon, Marianas.
(NAVY DEPT., NATIONAL ARCHIVES)

A twin-engined Japanese bomber goes down near the Kitkun Bay *near Saipan on the eve of the Marianas "Turkey Shoot."* (NAVY DEPT., NATIONAL ARCHIVES)

pilots to scramble and antiaircraft gunners to prepare their guns. Great rings of destroyers and cruisers, guns pointing skyward, had been formed around the carriers in four large groups spread over hundreds of square miles to the west of the Marianas.

The old American circus battle cry activated the carriers, and the Wildcats that had been over Guam turned about and raced out to sea. They would intercept the oncoming Japanese, but Guam continued to suffer under bombers and torpedo bombers. At 10:07 A.M. the ticker tape on the *Lexington* read: "Unidentified planes have been picked up bearing 333°, 45 miles away." Hellcats from the *Essex, Cowpens, Bunker Hill,* and *Princeton* vectored in upon the oncoming planes—the scouts and scout bombers of the Japanese 3rd Carrier Division. In the first skirmish, well to the west of the American carriers, about twenty-five Japanese planes (of seventy-three) were splashed into the sea. The survivors continued on resolutely, only to be met head on by another formation of Hellcats—sixteen more Japanese planes fell into the sea. Those still flying (about thirty) broke through the battle line (the battleships and destroyers that stood fifteen miles in the vanguard of the carrier formations). One of the bombers scored a direct hit upon the *South Dakota,* but not one Japanese plane reached the carriers. Of the original seventy-three only twenty-four survived for the time being. Some crash-landed on Guam and others returned to their own carriers.

The first large attack wave, the 129 fighters, bombers, and torpedo bombers of the 1st Carrier Division, were intercepted about an hour after the battle had begun. The Japanese planes ran head on into a mass of Hellcats, which shattered the formations—about a hundred planes fell before the carriers were reached. And the six of these which actually broke through were destroyed by savage antiaircraft fire or the combat air patrol planes circling the carriers.

Commander Ernest M. Snowden, of the *Lexington,* recalls how "We could see vapor trails of planes coming in with tiny black specks at the head. It was just like the skywriting we all used to see before the war. The sky was a white overcast and for some reason the planes were making vapor trails at a much lower altitude than usual. That made it easier for our boys to find the incoming Japs."

There were plenty of Japanese to go around, apparently. One young pilot, Ensign Bradford Hagie, found action even during a simple ferry flight. He had been forced to land on another carrier the previous day with engine trouble. Anxious to return to the *Lexington,* about three thousand yards away, he took off the next morning during what turned out to be the attack by the first wave. Hearing the radio chatter about the approaching unidentified aircraft, he remained air-borne for a while and on his way to the *Lexington* shot down three planes.

When the second, larger wave approached another young pilot sat gloomily in his Hellcat off to one side of the battle, circling out of the way because his engine was giving him trouble. He was Lieutenant Alexander Vraicu, and with his windscreen smeared with oil and his engine incapable of pulling at full power, he and five other "orphans" (planes with assorted problems but still flyable) orbited over the carriers. The decks had to be kept clear for takeoffs for the fighters.

Disappointed, Vraicu, who had gained much experience as a wingman of Butch O'Hare's, listened to the sounds of battle to the west on his radio. He heard the voice of the fighter director of the *Lexington* calling out vectors of approach.

"Vector 265." Vraicu turned the Hellcat in that direction, sharply squinting his eyes until he saw three forms in the sky coming his way. They proved to be the first of perhaps fifty planes, Zekes, Judys, and Jills. Other Hellcats began to race for the formation also. The air armadas met, converged, and then sprang apart into twisting individual air battles. Vraicu had forgotten about his engine trouble; the Japanese planes had ventured too close to the American carriers. Vraicu dived into the formation of Japanese bombers, opening up on the first plane in sight—a Judy. Within five seconds his voice was heard over the radio, "Scratch one Judy!"

Over the next few minutes Vraicu's guns sliced through one Judy after another, until his score for the single battle amounted to six. To the youthful pilot it seemed that there were simply too many planes to be taken care of, and that some came in dangerously close to the American ships. To his dismay he saw one lone Judy heading for a battleship, and he kicked his Hellcat around hoping to head off the bomber. But antiaircraft bursts came up and the Judy flew through the puffs for a few moments

Japanese ships dodging attacks from American carrier planes, June 19, 1944, the day of the "Turkey Shoot."
(NAVY DEPT., NATIONAL ARCHIVES)

and then flashed apart a thousand feet in the air.

Low on fuel, Vraicu returned to the *Lexington.* For some reason the gunners began shooting at him and Vraicu voiced his views on the ship's gunners as he circled and came in again for a landing. When his plane stopped, Vraicu stood up in the cockpit and held up six fingers. In eight minutes he had brought his total score up to nineteen.

A third Japanese raid was led astray by a faulty compass reading and missed most of the fighting. About a dozen of the forty-seven planes of the 2nd Carrier Division ran into Hellcats, which shot down seven. The remaining forty returned to their carriers.

When the fourth raid was launched, some of the spared pilots of the third raid joined it to make up a force of about eighty aircraft. This force too was led astray, but instead of returning to the carriers, the planes turned north, toward Guam, and ran into the Hellcats of the *Cabot, Wasp, Monterey,* and *Bunker Hill.* The day's slaughter continued in a whirl of dogfights—Japanese bombers attempting to get at the carriers were shot out of the air. Eighteen, met by Hellcats, were soon cut in half. The scattered survivors of the raid, forty-nine in all, were jumped over Guam as they attempted to find haven there. Thirty planes flared and fell; the remaining nineteen that finally landed, in various stages of distress, either crashed or were strafed into junk. Of the eighty planes which had left on the strike, nine returned to their home bases. The last

"Turkey Shoot" victor Alexander Vraicu of the Lexington *indicates his score during one battle in a Hellcat with a bad engine.*

(NAVY DEPT., NATIONAL ARCHIVES)

of the survivors of the day's battle fled for their carriers around six forty-five in the evening. The final battle of the Turkey Shoot occurred over Guam when four Hellcats, led by Lieutenant Commander C. W. Brewer over Orote Field, pounced a limping Jill attempting to land. Brewer's forces were in turn jumped by a large number of land-based Zekes, which had somehow eluded the day's bombings and strafings. Brewer was killed in this last battle of the day as darkness fell on the great battle arena.

The coming of night brought little comfort to Ozawa; he had no decisive victory to report. Two of his largest carriers were deep under the sea and 346 of his planes simply did not return to the carriers. And not one American plane had approached the Japanese carriers during the entire day. Toyoda, at Combined Fleet headquarters at Hiroshima, ordered Ozawa to withdraw before the Americans found his other carriers. Bitterly, Ozawa complied. He planned to refuel his ships and strike back with all he had on the next day.

Spruance then unleashed the straining Mitscher, who set off westward with three carrier groups, leaving one in the vicinity of the Marianas to continue creating a hell on earth on Guam and Rota. At

one o'clock on June 20, 1944, Ozawa transferred to the carrier *Zuikaku* (now the sole surviving veteran of the Hawaii Operation); he planned to strike again on the twenty-first. It appeared that he might have his way, for there was no sign of the American fleet. Search planes launched by Mitscher had not found the Japanese fleet either.

At one-thirty in the afternoon Lieutenant R. S. Nelson had taken off in an Avenger and set off on his search pattern. Two hours and ten minutes later, when he was about at the end of his tether, Nelson found what no one had yet found in the past several days: the Japanese fleet. He began sending a message back to the *Lexington,* but distance and weather garbled it and, although alerted, Mitscher was unable to make a decision. And in less than four hours he knew the sun would go down suddenly, as it did in the Pacific.

As Nelson continued sending messages they were picked up by the Japanese cruiser *Atago* nearby. They could only mean that the Americans had found the Japanese fleet. Ozawa was immediately notified and he ordered all refueling stopped and the ships away at twenty-four knots.

It took nearly fifteen minutes of sending before Nelson's contact report finally made any sense. Mitscher had already begun to make his plans, however. When Nelson's final, corrected position and disposition report came in at 4:05 P.M., Mitscher was prepared to launch his aircraft. But not without risk, for it was already late in the day and the Japanese ships were 275 miles away. It meant a long flight for them, then the battle and a long flight back.

"Taking advantage of this opportunity to destroy the Japanese fleet was going to cost us a great deal in planes and pilots because we were launching at the maximum range of our aircraft at such a time that it would be necessary to recover them after dark," Mitscher realized. "This meant that all carriers would be recovering daylight-trained air groups at night, with consequent loss of some pilots who were not familiar with night landings and who would be fatigued at the end of an extremely hazardous and long mission."

At four forty-one the carriers turned into the wind and ten minutes later no less than 216 planes were air-borne, 85 of them Hellcats. Two hours of flying brought them within sight of the Japanese ships.

Avenger pilot Lieutenant Ronald Gift of Marlette, Michigan, after a successful strike upon Japanese ships that had fled the shambles of the "Turkey Shoot." Gift's was one of the planes that was able to land in the dark when Mitscher canceled blackout regulations. The chalked message over Gift's head was the motto of Navy bomber pilots.

(NAVY DEPT., NATIONAL ARCHIVES)

Six oilers, left astern after Ozawa had ordered the ships away, were the first to come under attack. Dive bombers swept down and disabled two—*Genyo Maru* and *Seiyo Maru*—so thoroughly that they were abandoned and scuttled by evening.

One of the last messages the American pilots had seen as they raced from their ready rooms was chalked on the blackboards, "Get the CARRIERS." Worthy targets, the carriers were the prime objectives so far as most pilots were concerned. Leaving the transports burning and scattered, the carrier pilots continued their search for the Japanese carriers. Soon they came into view.

Lieutenant George B. Brown, Avenger pilot from the *Belleau Wood,* led seven other Avengers (four of them from the *Yorktown*), circled around the Japanese ships, and then selected the *Hiyo* to the port. The *Yorktown* Avengers split away and headed

to the starboard for the larger *Zuikaku* (now Ozawa's flagship), and the four *Belleau Wood* Avengers headed for the *Hiyo.* Antiaircraft fire was desperately heavy and Brown's Avenger was hit as he ran the plane in. He had not yet dropped his torpedo when a fragment of his left wing ripped away and flames filled the cockpit of the Avenger.

The Marianas prizes: in this reconnaissance photograph which spans a distance of twenty-six miles in a southwesterly direction, Saipan lies in the foreground. The airstrip near Marpi Point, Saipan's northernmost tip, is at the bottom of the photo. Aslito airfield is hidden under a cloud near top left of the picture. Across Saipan Channel lies Tinian with one of its two airstrips visible. With the conquest of the Marianas a new phase in the Pacific war would follow: B-29 operations from Saipan, Tinian, and Guam. (U. S. AIR FORCE)

The hazards of landing on a carrier deck under poor lighting conditions after combat. A Wildcat has come in, the pilot has misjudged his speed, or his arresting hook has not caught, and his plane does not stop until it ends up in the Pacific. Nor before it damages all other objects in its path. Mitscher's decision to turn on carrier landing lights helped to diminish the number of such landings. (NAVY DEPT., NATIONAL ARCHIVES)

The radioman and gunner bailed out, but Brown, who had said before taking off that he would get a carrier "at any cost," continued the run. The fire had burned itself out and Brown dropped his torpedo; his wingman, Lieutenant Benjamin Tate, dropped too but did not claim a hit. Lieutenant Warren Omark, however, placed a torpedo into the *Hiyo.*

Tate, harassed by two Zekes and with one gun shot out, ducked into a cloud and lost the Japanese fighters. He then joined up with Brown's badly shot-up Avenger. The plane moved erratically and Brown appeared to be bleeding badly. Then Tate lost sight of Brown. Omark, having eluded a Zeke and a couple of Vals, caught up with Brown and tried to guide him back to the American carrier positions. Brown finally disappeared in a cloud and was never seen again. His two crewmen, who had parachuted, were rescued the following day, safely floating in their life jackets. They had witnessed the death throes of the *Hiyo,* which sank about two hours after Brown and Omark had placed their torpedoes into the carrier.

There was fighting aloft too, for Ozawa had scraped together about seventy-five planes to meet the Hellcats, Avengers, and Helldivers. As the Hellcats fought off the Zekes, the bombers attacked and strafed other ships, among them the *Zuikaku,* which though badly hit was not sunk, the *Junyo, Ryuho,* and *Chiyoda* (all light carriers). In the heavy fighting sixty-five Japanese planes went down; American losses reached twenty, victims of fighters and antiaircraft.

When the day ended Ozawa's log noted the tragedy of the two days' fighting of what was officially known as the Battle of the Philippine Sea. "Surviving carrier air power," it was written, "35 aircraft operational." Though he wished to continue the battle, Ozawa canceled the order for a surface battle and ordered the ships back to Okinawa.

About 190 American planes turned away from the battle and headed for their home carriers. Many were shot up, most were low on fuel—and night had fallen an hour before the first plane appeared over the American carriers. Task Force 58 turned into the wind and the hard-bitten Mitscher made another vital decision that day. Earlier in the day he had risked his pilots and planes on a long-range strike and now he believed he owed them something. In defiance of all regulations, caution, and possible Japanese snoopers and submarines, he turned to Captain Arleigh Burke, his chief of staff, and said, "Turn on the lights."

"We had almost reached the force when we saw the lights come on," Lieutenant E. J. Lawton of the *Enterprise* recalled in describing the homecoming of the planes. "It is clear that the task force did all in its power to make it easier for us to get home. Lieutenant [V. Van] Eason led us in over the *Enterprise* but her deck was fouled for some time. We circled for a few minutes, watching the lights of the planes below fan out in the pattern of a landing circle. But there had been too much strain in the last five hours to reduce things to a pattern now; and inevitably, landing circles became crowded, intervals were lost and deck crashes occurred. Many planes—too many—announced that their gas was gone and they were going into the water. Others were caught short in the groove.

Japanese air power in the Marianas: a Marine grins down from a "meatball" on a Zeke wingtip at Aslito, Saipan. (U. S. NAVY)

"Seen from above, it was a weird kaleidoscope of fast-moving lights forming intricate trails in the darkness, punctuated now and then by tracers shooting through the night as someone landed with his gun switches on, and again by suddenly brilliant exhaust flames as each plane took a cut, or someone's turtleback light getting lower and lower until blacked out by the waves closing over it."

About 80 planes crashed or splashed into the water during the landing attempts. Rescue ships picked up 59 men; in all, 49 were lost, either in battle or because they sank in their aircraft before they could be rescued. The two days' total loss to the American fleet was 130 planes (compared to Ozawa's 480—this number includes both carrier- and land-base aircraft). Seventy-six American airmen perished in the Battle of the Philippine Sea, a fair trade, in the arithmetic of war, for hundreds of Japanese pilots and planes and three carriers.

The trade for the Marianas as future air bases

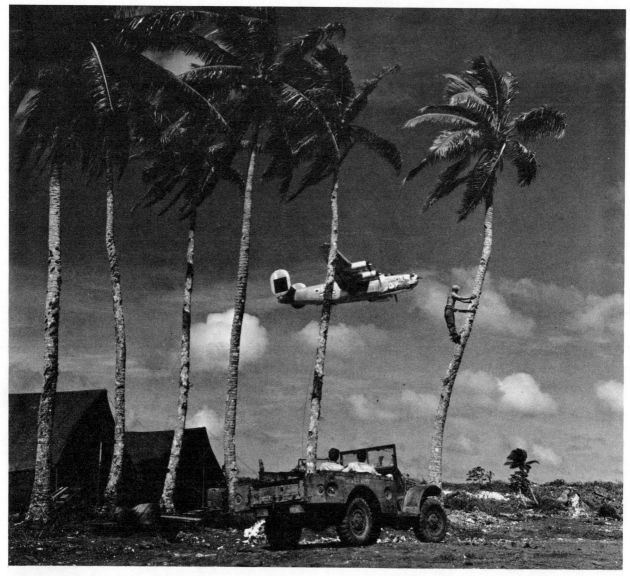

Guam secured: an 11th Bomb Group (Seventh Air Force) plane takes off for a mission from the Marianas *for strikes on the Bonins and Carolines.*

(U. S. AIR FORCE)

and harbors for ships and submarines was also worthwhile. Guam and Tinian fell by August 10 and the Marianas were officially declared "secure," although thousands of enemy troops in hiding had to be killed before the islands were completely free of fighting.

Political repercussions in Japan were nearly as drastic as the military defeat. General Tojo, who had scoffed at the thought of a Marianas invasion by the Americans, declared upon the fall of Saipan that "Japan is threatened by a national crisis with-out precedent." When the fall of Saipan was officially announced to the bewildered people of Japan, so was the fall of Tojo's cabinet. The Emperor, urged on by the *jushin* (elder statesmen without power who advised him), accepted the resignation of Tojo on July 18, 1944.

The Greater East Asia Co-Prosperity Sphere, which had swollen under Tojo's bellicose domination like some bloated balloon, had begun its inexorable collapse. The arrogant samurai had been diminished into just another turkey.

Index

Note: Page numbers in *italics* indicate illustrations